Contents

Meeting **SEN**
in the Curriculum:

DESIGN AND TECHNOLOGY

Louise T. Davies

 David Fulton Publishers

David Fulton Publishers Ltd
The Chiswick Centre, 414 Chiswick High Road, London W4 5TF

www.fultonpublishers.co.uk

10 9 8 7 6 5 4 3 2 1

Note: the right of Louise Davies to be identified as the author of this work has been asserted
by her in accordance with the Copyright, Designs and Patents Act 1988.

Copyright © Louise Davies 2004

British Library Cataloguing in Publication Data
A catalogue record for this book is available from the British Library.

David Fulton Publishers is a division of ITV plc.

ISBN 1 84312 166 2

Typeset by Servis Filmsetting Ltd, Manchester
Printed and bound in Great Britain

Acknowledgements

I am indebted to the following people who have helped me over many years towards this book:

Royal College of Art Schools Technology Project team – many of the ideas that were developed in 1996–97 but never published as 'Challenges Extra' form a basis for this book.

Design and Technology Association (DATA) SEN Advisory group members.

All the teachers who have attended Qualifications and Curriculum Authority (QCA) focus group meetings or allowed me to visit your schools. You told me how you adapt the activities for your pupils: we have a lot to learn from you about differentiation and individualising learning!

Those people who allowed me to use the work from their schools:

Steve Gilbert (formerly Wood Lane School) for the Pasties Case Study and sample worksheets in Chapter 5

Brian Russell (Dixon's CTC) for the Bolling Case Study in Chapter 5

Hugh Sammons (Queens Croft School) for the Working Together Week Case Study in Chapter 5 and the example D&T policy

Sue Stalley at Alexandra School for the P level 4 example in Chapter 6

Heather Wither at Mayfield School for the snack bars examples in Chapters 6 and 8

Donna Trebell from Wrotham School for the handheld technologies example in Chapter 8

Chris Killey from The Lindfield School for the vehicles project example in Chapter 8

Chris Clarke from West Of England School for the bread examples in Chapter 8 and examples of pupils using Braille and Wikki Stix®

Josie Brown from Wightwick Hall School for the lantern project in Chapter 8

Gary Drabble from All Saints RC School for the alarms project in Chapter 8

Mike Lewis at Giffard Park School for their example D&T scheme of work unit for puppets and puppets examples in Chapter 6

Photo / reproduction credits

KS3 National Strategy D&T pilot – for the KS3 checklist in Chapter 5
KS3 Strategy – SEN Training materials for the Foundation Subjects
© Crown copyright materials is reproduced with the permission of the Controller of HMSO and Queen's Printer

Roy Ballam at British Nutrition Foundation for the photo of set outs Chapter 7
©British Nutrition Foundation

Qualifications and Curriculum Authority *Including all Learners* checklist, P level descriptions, and KS3 SoW unit – 2B Puppets (© QCA 2000 Schemes of Work from the Standards Site at www.standards.dfee.gov.uk)

Disabled Living Foundation – for pictures of adapted equipment
©Disabled Living Foundation

Hodder and Stoughton for the use of the assessment grid for Puppets in Chapter 6
©Hodder and Stoughton

Roy Ballam, Louise Davies and Nikki Young for Technopacks ~SEN Design Sheets and certificate
©Technopacks

This book is dedicated to the very special staff and pupils at Aspen House School, London. Without you I would have left teaching in 1986 to sell microwave ovens. How much richer you made my world!

Contributors to the Series

The author

Louise T. Davies is part-time Policy Consultant for Design and Technology at QCA (Qualifications and Curriculum Authority), advising DfES on National Curriculum and examinations. In addition to this she is also a part-time free-lance D&T consultant. Recent consultancies inlcude: KS3 National Strategy Foundation Subjects – D&T pilot; Open University PGCE tutor; D&T adviser Thurrock LEA; senior lecturer for D&T PGCE at Brunel and Bath Spa Universities; Ofsted ITE additional inspector, Open University Learning Schools Programme. Currently, she is on the editorial board of the DATA journal, is chair of the DATA special needs advisory group, and external examiner for two university D&T teacher training courses. She provides much in-service training, has published over 40 D&T textbooks and edited a wide variety of resource materials. Her experience includes Deputy Project Director of the Royal College of Art Schools Technology Project, senior lecturer at South Bank University, senior management team and teacher in mainstream and special schools.

A dedicated team of SEN specialists and subject specialists have contributed to the *Meeting Special Needs in the Curriculum* series.

Series editor

Alan Combes started teaching in South Yorkshire in 1967 and was Head of English at several secondary schools before taking on the role of Head of PSHE as part of being senior teacher at Pindar School, Scarborough. He took early retirement to focus on his writing career and has authored two citizenship textbooks as well as writing several features for the *TES*. He has been used as an adviser on citizenship by the DfES and has emphasised citizenship's importance for special needs pupils as a speaker for NASEN.

SEN specialists

Sue Briggs is a freelance education consultant based in Hereford. She writes and speaks on inclusion, special educational needs and disability, and Autistic Spectrum Disorders and is a lay member of the SEN and Disability Tribunal. Until recently, she was SEN Inclusion Co-ordinator for Herefordshire Education Directorate. Originally trained as a secondary music teacher, Sue has extensive experience in mainstream and special schools. For six years she was teacher in charge of a language disorder unit.

Sue Cunningham is a learning support co-ordinator at a large mainstream secondary school in the West Midlands where she manages a large team of learning support teachers and assistants. She has experience of working in both mainstream and special schools and has set up and managed a resource base for pupils with moderate learning difficulties in the mainstream as part of an initiative to promote a more inclusive education for pupils with SEN.

Sally McKeown is an Education Officer with Becta, the government funded agency responsible for managing the National Grid for Learning. She is responsible for the use of IT for learners with disabilities, learning difficulties or additional needs. She is a freelance journalist for the *Times Educational Supplement* and a regular contributor to disability magazines and to *Special Children* magazine. In 2001 her book *Unlocking Potential* was shortlisted for the NASEN Special Needs Book Award.

Subject specialists

English

Tim Hurst has been a special educational needs co-ordinator in five schools and is particularly interested in the role and use of language in teaching.

Science

Carol Holden works as a science teacher and assistant SENCO in a mainstream secondary school. She has developed courses for pupils with SEN within science and has gained a graduate diploma and MA in Educational Studies, focusing on SEN.

History

Richard Harris has been teaching since 1989. He has taught in three comprehensive schools, as history teacher, Head of Department and Head of Faculty. He has also worked as teacher consultant for secondary history in West Berkshire.

Ian Luff is Assistant Headteacher of Kesgrave High School, Suffolk and has been Head of History in three comprehensive schools.

Maths

Brian Sharp is a Key Stage 3 Mathematics consultant for Herefordshire. Brian has long experience of working both in special and mainstream schools as a teacher of mathematics. He has a range of management experience, including SENCO, mathematics and ICT co-ordinator.

Religious education

Dilwyn Hunt has worked as a specialist RE adviser, first in Birmingham and now in Dudley. He has a wide range of experience in the teaching of RE, including mainstream and special RE.

Music

Victoria Jaquiss is SEN specialist for music with children with emotional and behavioural difficulties in Leeds. She devised a system of musical notation primarily for use with steel pans, for which, in 2002, she was awarded the fellowship of the Royal Society of Arts.

Diane Paterson works as an inclusive music curriculum teacher in Leeds.

Geography

Diane Swift is a project leader for the Geographical Association. Her interest in special needs developed whilst she was a Staffordshire geography adviser and inspector.

PE and sport

Crispin Andrews is an education/sports writer with nine years' experience of teaching and sports coaching.

Art

Kim Earle is Able Pupils Consultant for St Helens and has been a Head of Art and Design. Kim is also a practising designer jeweller.

Gill Curry is Gifted and Talented Strand Co-ordinator for the Wirral. She has twenty years' experience as Head of Art and has also been an art advisory teacher. She is also a practising artist specialising in print.

ICT

Mike North works for ICTC, an independent consultancy specialising in the effective use of ICT in education. He develops educational materials and provides advice and support for the SEN sector.

Sally McKeown is an Education Officer with Becta, the government funded agency responsible for managing the National Grid for Learning and the FERL website. She is responsible for the use of IT for learners with disabilities, learning difficulties or additional needs.

Citizenship

Alan Combes started teaching in South Yorkshire in 1967 and was Head of English at several secondary schools before taking on the role of Head of PSHE as part of being senior teacher at Pindar School, Scarborough. He took early retirement to focus on his writing career and has authored two citizenship textbooks as well as writing several features for the TES. He has been used as an adviser on citizenship by the DfES and has emphasised citizenship's importance for special needs pupils as a speaker for NASEN.

Modern foreign languages

Sally McKeown is responsible for language-based work in the Inclusion team at Becta. She has a particular interest in learning difficulties and dyslexia. She writes regularly for the *TES, Guardian* and *Special Children* magazine.

Contents of the CD

The CD contains activities and record sheets which can be amended/individualised and printed out for use by the purchasing institution.

Increasing the font size and spacing will improve accessibility for some students, as will changes in background colour. Alternatively, print onto pastel-coloured paper for greater ease of reading.

Contents of the CD

Introduction

All children have the right to a good education and the opportunity to fulfil their potential. All teachers should expect to teach children with special educational needs (SEN) and all schools should play their part in educating children from the local community, whatever their background or ability. *Removing Barriers to Achievement: The Government's Strategy for SEN*, Feb. 2004

A raft of legislation and statutory guidance over the past few years has sought to make our mainstream education system more inclusive and ensure that pupils with a diverse range of ability and need are well catered for. This means that all staff need to have an awareness of how children learn and develop in different ways, and an understanding of how barriers to achievement can be removed – or at least minimised.

These barriers often result from inappropriate teaching styles, inaccessible teaching materials or ill-advised grouping of pupils, as much as from an individual child's physical, sensory or cognitive impairments: a fact which is becoming better understood. It is this developing understanding that is now shaping the legislative and advisory landscape of our education system, and making it necessary for all teachers to reconsider carefully their curriculum planning and classroom practice.

The major statutory requirements and non-statutory guidance are summarised in Chapter 1, setting the context for this resource and providing useful starting points for departmental INSET.

It is clear that provision for pupils with special educational needs (SEN) is not the sole responsibility of the special educational needs co-ordinator (SENCO) and her team of assistants. If, in the past, subject teachers have 'taken a back seat' in the planning and delivery of a suitable curriculum for these children and expected the learning support department to bridge the gap between what was on offer in the classroom or workshop, and what they actually needed – they can no longer do so. *The Code of Practice* (2002), states that:

> All teaching and non teaching staff should be involved in the development of the school's SEN policy and be fully aware of the school's procedure for identifying, assessing and making provision for pupils with SEN.

Chapter 2 looks at departmental policy for SEN provision and provides useful audit material for reviewing and developing current practice.

The term 'special educational needs' or SEN is now widely used and has become something of a catch-all descriptor – rendering it less than useful in many cases. Before the Warnock Report (1978) and subsequent introduction of the term 'special educational needs', any pupils who for whatever reason (cognitive difficulties, emotional and behavioural difficulties, speech and language disorders) progressed more slowly than the 'norm' were designated 'remedials' and grouped together in the bottom sets without the benefit, in many cases, of specialist subject teachers .

But the SEN tag was also applied to pupils in special schools who had more significant needs and who had previously been identified as 'disabled' or even 'uneducable'. Add to these the deaf pupils, those with impaired vision, others with mobility problems, and even children from other countries, with a limited understanding of the English language – who may or may not have been highly intelligent – and you had a recipe for confusion, to say the least.

The day-to-day descriptors used in the staffroom are gradually being moderated and refined as greater knowledge and awareness of special needs is built up. (We still hear staff describing pupils as 'totally thick', a 'nutcase' or 'complete moron' – but hopefully only as a means of letting off steam!) However, there are terms in common use which, though more measured and well-meaning, can still be unhelpful and misleading. Teachers will describe a child as being 'dyslexic' when they mean that he is poor at reading and writing; 'ADHD' has become a synonym for badly behaved; and a child who seems to be withdrawn or just eccentric is increasingly described as 'autistic'.

The whole process of applying labels is fraught with danger, but sharing a common vocabulary – and more importantly, a common understanding – can help colleagues to express their concerns about a pupil and address the issues as they appear in the design and technology workshop or classroom. Often, this is better achieved by identifying the particular areas of difficulty experienced by the pupil rather than puzzling over what syndrome he may have. The Code of Practice identifies four main areas of difficulty and these are detailed in Chapter 3 – along with an 'at a glance' guide to a wide range of syndromes and conditions and guidance on how they might present barriers to learning.

There is no doubt that the number of children with special needs being educated in mainstream schools is growing:

> . . . because of the increased emphasis on the inclusion of children with SEN in mainstream schools the number of these children is increasing, as are the severity and variety of their SEN. Children with a far wider range of learning difficulties and variety of medical conditions, as well as sensory difficulties and physical disabilities, are now attending mainstream classes. The implication of this is that mainstream school teachers need to expand their knowledge and skills with regard to the needs of children with SEN. (Stakes and Hornby 2000:3)

The continuing move to greater inclusion means that all teachers can now expect to teach pupils with varied, and quite significant, SEN at some time. Even five years ago, it was rare to come across children with Asperger's/Down's/Tourette's Syndrome, Autistic Spectrum Disorder or significant physical/sensory disabilities in community secondary schools. Now, they are entering mainstream education in growing numbers and there is a realisation that their 'inclusion' cannot be simply the responsibility of the SENCO and support staff. All staff have to be aware of particular learning needs and able to employ strategies in the classroom and workshop that directly address those needs.

Chapter 4 considers the components of an inclusive classroom and how the physical environment and resources, structure of the lesson and teaching approaches can make a real difference to pupils with special needs. This theme is extended in Chapter 5 to look more closely at teaching and learning styles and consider ways in which to help all pupils maximise their potential.

The monitoring of pupils' achievements and progress is a key factor in identifying and meeting their learning needs. Those pupils who make slower progress than their peers are often working just as hard, or even harder, but their efforts can go unrewarded. Chapter 6 addresses the importance of target setting and subsequent assessment and review in acknowledging pupils' achievements and in showing the department's effectiveness in value-added terms.

Liasing with the SENCO and support staff is an important part of every teacher's role. The SENCO's status in a secondary school often means that this teacher is part of the leadership team and influential in shaping whole-school policy and practice. Specific duties might include:

- ensuring liaison with parents and other professionals

- advising and supporting teaching and support staff

- ensuring that appropriate Individual Education Plans are in place

- ensuring that relevant background information about individual children with special educational needs is collected, recorded and updated

- making plans for future support and setting targets for improvement

- monitoring and reviewing action taken

The SENCO has invariably undergone training in different aspects of special needs provision and has much to offer colleagues in terms of in-house training and advice about appropriate materials to use with pupils. Though often overlooked in this capacity, the SENCO should be a frequent and valuable point of reference for all staff. The SENCO's presence at the occasional departmental meeting can be very effective in developing teachers' skills in relation to meeting SEN, making them aware of new initiatives and methodology and sharing information about individual children.

In most schools however, the SENCO's skills and knowledge are channelled to the chalkface via a team of Teaching or Learning Support Assistants (TAs, LSAs). These assistants can be very able and well-qualified, but very underused in the classroom. Chapter 7 looks at how teachers can manage in-class support in a way that makes the best use of a valuable resource.

Describing real-life situations with real pupils is a powerful way to demonstrate ideas and guidance. In Chapter 8, a number of case-studies illustrate how different approaches can work.

The revised regulations for SEN provision make it clear that mainstream schools are expected to provide for pupils with a wide diversity of needs, and teaching is evaluated on the extent to which all pupils are engaged and enabled to achieve.

This book has been produced in response to the implications of all of this for secondary subject teachers. It has been written by a national D&T specialist with support from colleagues who have expertise within the SEN field so that the information and guidance given is both subject specific and pedagogically sound. The book and accompanying CD provide a resource that can be used with colleagues:

- to shape departmental policy and practice for special needs provision

- enable staff to react with a measured response when inclusion issues arise

- ensure that every pupil achieves appropriately in D&T.

Meeting Special Educational Needs – Your Responsibility

Inclusion in education involves the process of increasing the participation of students in, and reducing their exclusion from, the cultures, curricula and communities of local schools. (*The Index for Inclusion* 2000)

The Index for Inclusion was distributed to all maintained schools by the Department for Education and Skills and has been a valuable tool for many schools as they have worked to develop their inclusive practice. It supports schools in the review of their policies, practices and procedures, and the development of an inclusive approach and, where it has been used as part of the school improvement process – looking at inclusion in the widest sense – it has been a great success. For many people, however, the *Index* lacked any real teeth, and recent legislation and non-statutory guidance is more authoritative.

The SEN and Disability Act 2001 (SENDA)

The SEN and Disability Act amended the Disability Discrimination Act and created important new duties for schools. Under this Act, schools are obliged:

- to take reasonable steps to ensure that disabled pupils are not placed at a substantial disadvantage in relation to the education and other services they provide. This means they must anticipate where barriers to learning lie and take action to remove them as far as they are able

- to plan strategically to increase the extent to which disabled pupils can participate in the curriculum, make the physical environment more accessible and ensure that written material is provided in accessible formats

The reasonable steps taken might include:

- changing policies and practices

- changing course requirements

- changing the physical features of a building

- providing interpreters or other support workers

- delivering courses in alternative ways

- providing materials in other formats

The staff in the design and technology department should produce all their worksheets (for example, designing sheets, research information) and activities in electronic form so that they can be easily converted into large print, or put into other alternative formats, such as Braille or supported word processing (with speech feedback, predictive text, or on screen grids) or symbols. In electronic format it is easy to produce sheets at levels appropriate to ability with minor changes.

The department should plan and review the activities planned each year and consider further what technological aids can be provided to give specific support in some practical activities, for example posture aids, and specialist equipment such as talking weighing scales, computer-aided manufacturing (CAM).

Appendix 1 on the CD which accompanies this book provides an activity involving departmental discussion of inclusion, and Appendix 2.2 gives further detail on SENDA and a related activity.

The Revised National Curriculum

The Revised National Curriculum (2002) emphasises the provision of effective learning opportunities for all learners and establishes three principles for promoting inclusion:

- setting suitable learning challenges

- responding to pupils' diverse learning needs

- overcoming potential barriers to learning and assessment

The National Curriculum Inclusion Statement sets out requirements and opportunities for teachers to adapt and adjust the National Curriculum to provide effective learning experiences for all pupils. It has a general statement that applies to all subjects and additional subject-specific information for each National Curriculum subject. (Please see National Curriculum D&T document pp. 28–36). It contains specific examples to consider for D&T to help implement the statutory inclusion statement – on the basis of religious beliefs, gender, and pupils with disabilities. Schools can use this to legitimise modifications to the Programme of Study, to gain reassurance that their teaching approaches are appropriate, to give clarity to Ofsted inspectors and senior managers and to gain effective specialist resources (such as CAD/CAM) to meet the needs of the pupils.

For example, it states that to overcome potential barriers, some pupils may require:

- alternative or adapted activities to overcome difficulties with tools, equipment and materials, for example use CAD/CAM, or another person as a helper *to support aspects of the Programme of Study that deal with making*

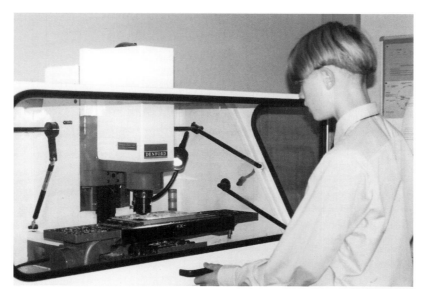

Using a CAD/CAM machine to overcome barriers in making

- technological aids or specialist software to help with sequencing and following instructions *to support aspects of the Programme of Study that deal with designing, communicating and making*

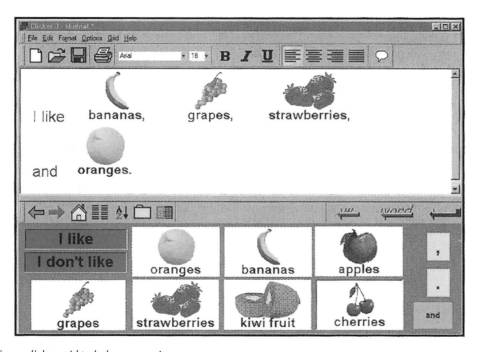

Using a clicker grid to help sequencing

- opportunities to communicate through means other than writing or drawing to help them record or translate their design ideas into a drawing *to support aspects of the Programme of Study that deal with designing, and recording work*

- more time than others to complete the range of work indicated in the Breadth of Study statement, for example doing shorter assignments, by combining experience in more than one material in an assignment

Including all learners in D&T

The National Curriculum guidance suggests that staff may need to differentiate tasks and materials, and facilitate access to learning by, for example:

SETTING SUITABLE LEARNING CHALLENGES

Some pupils will learn more effectively through being presented more structured or limited tasks in familiar contexts. Teachers can provide for this, for example by allowing pupils to:

- undertake design and make assignments (DMAs) in contexts with which they are familiar or work on tasks related to their hobbies, interests and strengths
- adapt, make improvements, or add a new feature to the design of a product rather than invent a whole new product
- design a product where they are given alternative solutions (it is important to avoid tokenism – there should still be an opportunity for real designing)

RESPONDING TO PUPILS' DIVERSE LEARNING NEEDS

Some pupils who progress more slowly will need opportunities to complete a task and achieve success. Through planning and a teaching approach, teachers can, for example:

- encourage a minimum coverage of the range of materials and contexts in the units, but provide fewer opportunities to revisit them
  For example *Use only one unit which focuses on control rather than three*
- allow pupils to engage only in the most relevant parts of the design process
  Teachers could provide some research for a project so that pupils concentrate on analysis
- use shorter, more focused DMAs, rather than longer open ones, in order to provide incremental elements of success
- combine experience in more than one material in a DMA, such as wood, plastic and food

---

OVERCOMING POTENTIAL BARRIERS

Pupils with difficulties in communication, language and literacy
To ensure that these pupils attain the highest standards, ensure the scheme meets their requirements, for example by:

- using, where appropriate and available, means of communication other than writing or drawing (for example, a pupil may describe their design ideas for others to record or translate into a drawing, while retaining control of the design idea and modifications)
- supporting (for example, through use of frameworks and language stems, through preparing and highlighting website pages) pupils' research, reading and writing assignments and reducing, where appropriate, the amount and complexity of writing, reading and research required
- giving pupils the opportunity to clarify their ideas through discussion, modelling, role play, tape recorders, video and photographs, rather than relying solely on writing
- using alternative and augmentative communication (for example, signing and symbolic recording system, where appropriate)
- providing ICT applications, for example CAD and specialist software, to help with sequencing and following instructions, software to allow direct voice input into word processing, and audio and video conferencing to enable teamwork on design products

Pupils with disabilities, sensory impairments or ill health
Enable pupils to participate fully, particularly in practical activities, for example by:

- providing alternative or adapted activities for pupils who are unable to manipulate tools, equipment or materials (for example, the use of CAD/CAM to produce quality products)
- providing specific support (for example, technological aids). These are specific to the needs of the individual pupil but may include specialist software, talking weighing scales, sensors, light probes and posture aids
- supporting pupils to enable them to participate safely in practical work (for example, the assistance of others to help pupils to hold or manipulate tools, or to carry out activities according to the instructions of the pupil). It is important that the pupil should retain control of the making process and be the decision maker
- identifying tasks with early achievable goals within a larger project to allow pupils suffering from illness, trauma or stress to engage with the work or to allow for the slower pace at which some pupils will complete their work, for example *during the DMA*
- providing opportunities for pupils to gain understanding about, and to evaluate, different products through non-visual means (for example, allowing tactile responses to products), for example *during product evaluation activities*
- providing for the use of non-visual or non-aural ways for pupils to acquire information when researching products or providing contexts to generate ideas, for example *during product evaluation activities and FPTs*

Performance levels below level 1

The Qualifications and Curriculum Authority (QCA) have also introduced performance descriptions (P levels/P scales) to enable teachers to observe and record small steps of progress made by some pupils with SEN. These descriptions outline early learning and attainment for each subject in the National Curriculum, including citizenship, RE and PSHE. They chart progress up to NC level 1 through eight steps. The performance descriptions for P1 to P3 are common across all subjects and outline the types and range of general performance that some pupils with learning difficulties might characteristically demonstrate. From level P4 onwards, many believe it is possible to describe performance in a way that indicates the emergence of subject-focused skills, knowledge and understanding.

There is more information on P levels in Chapter 6.

The Code of Practice for Special Educational Needs

The Revised Code of Practice (implemented in 2002) describes a cyclical process of planning, target setting and review for pupils with SEN. It also makes clear the expectation that the vast majority of pupils with special needs will be educated in mainstream settings. Those identified as needing over and above what the school can provide from its own resources, however, are nominated for 'School Action Plus', and outside agencies will be involved in planned intervention. This may involve professionals from the Learning Support Service, a specialist teacher or therapist, or an educational psychologist, working with the school's SENCO to put together an Individual Education Plan (IEP) for the pupil. In a minority of cases (the numbers vary widely between LEAs) pupils may be assessed by a multi-disciplinary team on behalf of the local education authority whose representatives then decide whether or not to issue a statement of SEN. This is a legally binding document detailing the child's needs and setting out the resources which should be provided. It is reviewed every year.

FUNDAMENTAL PRINCIPLES OF THE SPECIAL NEEDS CODE OF PRACTICE:

- A child with special educational needs should have their needs met.
- The special educational needs of children will normally be met in mainstream schools or settings.
- The views of the child should be sought and taken into account.
- Parents have a vital role to play in supporting their child's education.
- Children with special educational needs should be offered full access to a broad, balanced and relevant education, including an appropriate curriculum for the Foundation stage and the National Curriculum.

Ofsted

Ofsted inspectors are required to make judgements about a school's inclusion policy, and how it is translated into practice in individual classrooms. According to Ofsted (2003), the following key factors help schools to become more inclusive:

- a climate of acceptance of all pupils

- careful preparation of placements for SEN pupils

- availability of sufficient suitable teaching and personal support

- widespread awareness among staff of the particular needs of SEN pupils and an understanding of the practical ways of meeting these needs in the classroom

- sensitive allocation to teaching groups and careful curriculum modification, timetables and social arrangements

- availability of appropriate materials and teaching aids and adapted accommodation

- an active approach to personal and social development, as well as to learning

- well-defined and consistently applied approaches to managing difficult behaviour

- assessment, recording and reporting procedures which can embrace and express adequately the progress of pupils with more complex SEN who make only small gains in learning and PSD

- involving parents/carers as fully as possible in decision-making, keeping them well informed about their child's progress and giving them as much practical support as possible

- developing and taking advantage of training opportunities, including links with special schools and other schools

Policy into practice

Effective teaching for pupils with SEN is, by and large, effective for all pupils, but as schools become more inclusive, teachers need to be able to respond to a wider range of needs. The Government's strategy for SEN (*Removing Barriers to Learning*, 2004) sets out ambitious proposals to 'help teachers expand their repertoire of inclusive skills and strategies and plan confidently to include children with increasingly complex needs'.

In many cases, pupils' individual needs will be met through greater differentiation of tasks and materials, i.e. school-based intervention as set out in the SEN Code of Practice. A smaller number of pupils may need access to specialist equipment and approaches or to alternative or adapted activities, as part of a School Action Plus programme, augmented by advice and support from external specialists. The QCA, on its website (2003), encourages teachers to take specific action to provide access to learning for pupils with special educational needs by:

(a) providing for pupils who need help with communication, language and literacy, through:

- using texts that pupils can read and understand

- using visual and written materials in different formats, including large print, symbol text and Braille

- using ICT, other technological aids and taped materials

- using alternative and augmentative communication, including signs and symbols

- using translators, communicators and amanuenses

(b) planning, where necessary, to develop pupils' understanding through the use of all available senses and experiences by:

- using materials and resources that pupils can access through sight, touch, sound, taste or smell

- using word descriptions and other stimuli to make up for a lack of first-hand experiences

- using ICT, visual and other materials to increase pupils' knowledge of the wider world

- encouraging pupils to take part in everyday activities such as play, drama, class visits and exploring the environment

(c) planning for pupils' full participation in learning and in physical and practical activities by:

- using specialist aids and equipment

- providing support from adults or peers when needed

- adapting tasks or environments

- providing alternative activities, where necessary

(d) helping pupils to manage their behaviour, to take part in learning effectively and safely, and, at Key Stage 4, to prepare for work by:

- setting realistic demands and stating them explicitly

- using positive behaviour management, including a clear structure of rewards and sanctions

- giving pupils every chance and encouragement to develop the skills they need to work well with a partner or a group

- teaching pupils to value and respect the contribution of others

- encouraging and teaching independent working skills

- teaching essential safety rules

(e) helping individuals to manage their emotions, particularly trauma or stress, and to take part in learning by:

- identifying aspects of learning in which the pupil will engage and plan short-term, easily achievable goals in selected activities

- providing positive feedback to reinforce and encourage learning and build self-esteem

- selecting tasks and materials sensitively to avoid unnecessary stress for the pupil

- creating a supportive learning environment in which the pupil feels safe and is able to engage with learning

- allowing time for the pupil to engage with learning, and gradually increasing the range of activities and demands

Pupils with disabilities

The QCA goes on to provide guidance on pupils with disabilities, pointing out that not all pupils with disabilities will necessarily have SEN. Many learn alongside their peers with little need for additional resources beyond the aids which they use as part of their daily life, such as a wheelchair, a hearing aid or equipment to aid vision. Teachers' planning must ensure, however, that these pupils are enabled to participate as fully and effectively as possible in the curriculum by:

- planning appropriate amounts of time to allow for the satisfactory completion of tasks. This might involve:
  - taking account of the very slow pace at which some pupils will be able to record work, either manually or with specialist equipment, and of the physical effort required
  - being aware of the high levels of concentration necessary for some pupils when following or interpreting text or graphics, particularly when using vision aids or tactile methods, and of the tiredness which may result
  - allocating sufficient time, opportunity and access to equipment for pupils

to gain information through experimental work and detailed observation, including the use of microscopes

- being aware of the effort required by some pupils to follow oral work, whether through use of residual hearing, lip reading or a signer, and of the tiredness or loss of concentration which may occur

- planning opportunities, where necessary, for the development of skills in practical aspects of the curriculum. This might involve:
  - providing alternative or adapted activities in design and technology for pupils who are unable to manipulate tools, equipment or materials or who may be allergic to certain types of materials

- identifying aspects of programmes of study and attainment targets that may present specific difficulties for individuals. This might involve:
  - helping visually impaired pupils to evaluate different products in design and technology

The success of design and technology

In general, teachers of pupils with SEN welcome the opportunities offered by National Curriculum D&T to consolidate the learning of skills which are not so readily accessible in other subjects:

D&T makes a crucial contribution to the development of pupils' practical and thinking skills, and their ability to manufacture products, using a range of materials, tools equipment and techniques. It is this essentially practical aspect that makes D&T an attractive and valuable learning experience and environment for pupils of all abilities. D&T enables pupils to draw upon knowledge and understanding from across the curriculum as well as from D&T, and to apply this in a very practical way. For this reason D&T is extremely valuable to the learning and progress of pupils with SEN. (Curriculum Council for Wales 1993)

Pupils with SEN make better progress in D&T than in most other subjects. Pupils enjoy the practical application and can see the results of their efforts easily. The projects and lesson lend themselves to effective differentiation:

In the vast majority of lessons, provision for pupils with special educational needs (SEN) is satisfactory and it is good in over half of schools. (Ofsted subject reports 2002/03 *Design and Technology in Secondary Schools*, February 2004)

Ofsted noted, however, that while the commonly used technique of tightly structuring projects to support pupils with SEN works in many cases, it can also mean that pupils have fewer opportunities to extend their work and be creative:

Carefully organised projects enable pupils to make progress in Years 7 to 9 in researching, planning and testing, as well as in making. Teachers manage the projects well to control pace and productivity. Tightly structured projects are especially effective in supporting average pupils and those with SEN, although, when adhered to rigidly, they can discourage abler pupils from being innovative or exploring areas of interest in depth. Effective departments overcome this tendency by, for example:

> providing a broad range of opportunities for designing and making, which are well selected and enthusiastically introduced to capture the interests of the pupils. They are well balanced to cover the full range of D&T activities including strong elements of systems, control, pneumatics and electronics, with the underlying technological knowledge rigorously taught and carefully applied in project work. A wide range of materials is used with precision and a developing understanding of their properties.

Summary

Pupils with a wide range of needs – physical/sensory, emotional, cognitive and social – are present in increasing numbers, in all mainstream settings. Government policies point the way, with inclusion at the forefront of national policy – but it is up to teachers to make the rhetoric a reality. Teachers are ultimately responsible for all the children they teach. In terms of participation, achievement, enjoyment – the buck stops here!

Departmental Policy

It is crucial that departmental policy describes a strategy for meeting pupils' SEN within the particular curricular area. The policy should set the scene for any visitor to the design and technology department – from supply staff to inspectors – and make a valuable contribution to the departmental handbook. The process of developing a department SEN policy offers the opportunity to clarify and evaluate current thinking and practice within the design and technology team and to establish a consistent approach.

The policy should:

- clarify the responsibilities of all staff and identify any with specialist training and/or knowledge

- describe the curriculum on offer and how it can be differentiated

- outline arrangements for assessment and reporting

- guide staff on how to work effectively with support staff

- identify staff training

The starting point will be the school's SEN policy as required by the Education Act 1996, with each subject department 'fleshing out' the detail in a way which describes how things work in practice. The writing of a policy should be much more than a paper exercise completed to satisfy the senior management team and Ofsted inspectors: it is an opportunity for staff to come together as a team and create a framework for teaching design and technology in a way that makes it accessible to all pupils in the school.

The backdrop to writing the policy should be the National Curriculum statement for design and technology and the policy will set out how it can be achieved in practice for all pupils:

Design and technology prepares pupils to participate in tomorrow's rapidly changing technologies. They learn to think and intervene creatively to improve the quality of life. The subject calls for pupils to become autonomous and creative problem-solvers, as individuals and as members of a team. They must look for needs, wants and opportunities and respond to them by developing a range of ideas and making products and systems. They combine practical skills with an understanding of aesthetics, social and environmental issues, function and industrial practices. As they do so, they reflect on and evaluate present and past design and technology, its uses and effects. Through design and technology, all pupils can become discriminating and informed users of products, and become innovators. (*Design and technology – the National Curriculum for England*, DfEE, QCA, 1999: 15)

Where to start when writing a policy

An audit can act as a starting point for reviewing current policy on SEN or can inform the writing of a new policy. It will involve gathering information and reviewing current practice with regard to pupils with SEN and is best completed by the whole of the department, preferably with some additional advice from the SENCO or another member of staff with responsibility for SEN within the school. An audit carried out by the whole department can provide a valuable opportunity for professional developmental if it is seen as an exercise in sharing good practice and encouraging joint planning. But before embarking on an audit, it is worth investing some time in a department meeting or training day, to raise awareness of special educational needs legislation and establish a shared philosophy. Appendices 1 and 2.1 in the CD which accompanies this book contain activities to use with staff. The sheet published by QCA (see Appendix 2.2 on the CD) entitled *Including all learners* also raises awareness and can be a starting point for thinking about the issues. (See Appendix 2.3 for a sample D&T policy, and Appendix 2.4 for a DfEE document on the relevance of D&T to pupils with severe learning difficulties.)

The following headings may be useful in establishing a working policy:

General statement

- What does legislation and DfES guidance say?
- What does the school policy state?
- What do members of the department have to do to comply with it?

Definition of SEN

- What does SEN mean?
- What are the areas of need and the categories used in the Code of Practice?
- Are there any special implications within the subject area?

Provision for staff within the department

- How is information shared?
- Who has responsibility for SEN within the department?
- How and when is information shared?
- Where and what information is stored?

Provision for pupils with SEN

- How are pupils with SEN assessed and monitored in the department?
- How are contributions to IEPs and reviews made?
- What criteria are used for organising teaching groups?
- What alternative courses are offered to pupils with SEN?
- What special internal and external examination arrangements are made?
- What guidance is available for working with support staff?

Resources and learning materials

- Is there any specialist equipment used in the department?
- How are resources developed?
- Where are resources stored?

Staff qualifications and Continuing Professional Development needs

- What qualifications do the members of the department have?
- What training has taken place?
- How is training planned?
- Is a record kept of training completed and training needs?

Monitoring and reviewing the policy

- How will the policy be monitored?
- When will the policy be reviewed?

The content of an SEN departmental policy

This section gives detailed information on what an SEN policy might include. Each heading is expanded with some detailed information and raises the main issues with regard to teaching pupils with SEN. At the end of each section there is an example statement. The example statements can be personalised and brought together to make a policy. (A sample D&T policy can be seen in Appendix 2.3 on the CD.)

General statement with reference to the school's SEN policy

All schools must have an SEN policy according to the Education Act 1996. This policy will set out basic information on the school's SEN provision, and how the school identifies, assesses and provides for pupils with SEN, including information on staffing and working in partnership with other professionals and parents. Any department policy needs to have reference to the school SEN policy.

Example

> All members of the department will ensure that the needs of all pupils with SEN are met according to the aims of the school and its SEN policy.

Definition of SEN

It is useful to insert at least the four areas of SEN in the department policy, as used in the Code of Practice for Special Educational Needs.

Example

TABLE 2.1 DIFFERENT TYPES OF SEN

Cognition and Learning Needs	Behavioural, Emotional and Social Development Needs	Communication and Interaction Needs	Sensory and/or Physical Needs
Specific learning difficulties (SpLD)	Behavioural, emotional and social difficulties (BESD)	Speech, language and communication needs	Hearing impairment (HI)
Dyslexia	Attention Deficit Disorder (ADD)	Autistic Spectrum Disorder (ASD)	Visual impairment (VI)
Moderate learning difficulties (MLD)		Asperger's Syndrome	Multi-sensory impairment (MSI)
	Attention Deficit Hyperactivity Disorder (ADHD)		
Severe learning difficulties (SLD)			Physical difficulties (PD)
Profound and multiple learning difficulties (PMLD)			OTHER

Provision for staff within the department

In many schools, each department nominates a member of staff to have special responsibility for SEN provision (with or without remuneration). This can be very effective where there is a system of regular liaison between department SEN representatives and the SENCO in the form of meetings or paper communications or a mixture of both.

The responsibilities of this post may include liaison between the department and the SENCO, attending any liaison meetings and providing feedback via meetings and minutes, attending training, maintaining the departmental SEN information and records and representing the needs of pupils with SEN at departmental level. This post can be seen as a valuable development opportunity for staff. The name of this person should be included in the policy.

How members of the department raise concerns about pupils with SEN can be included in this section. Concerns may be raised at specified departmental meetings before referral to the SENCO. An identified member of the department could make referrals to the SENCO and keep a record of this information.

Reference to working with support staff will include a commitment to planning and communication between staff. There may be information on inviting support staff to meetings, resources and lesson plans.

A reference to the centrally held lists of pupils with SEN and other relevant information will also be included in this section. A note about confidentiality of information should be included.

Example

> The member of staff with responsibility for overseeing the provision of SEN within the department will attend liaison meetings and feed back to other members of the department. He will maintain the department's SEN information file, attend appropriate training and disseminate this to all departmental staff. All information will be treated with confidentiality.

Provision for pupils with SEN

It is the responsibility of all staff to know which pupils have SEN and to identify any pupils having difficulties. Pupils with SEN may be identified by staff within the department in a variety of ways, these may be listed and could include:

- observation in lessons
- assessment of class work
- homework tasks
- end of module tests
- progress checks

- annual examinations

- reports

Setting out how pupils with SEN are grouped within the design and technology department may include specifying the criteria used and/or the philosophy behind the method of grouping.

Example

> The pupils are grouped according to ability as informed by Key Stage 2 results, reading scores and any other relevant performance, social or medical information.
>
> Monitoring arrangements and details of how pupils can move between groups should also be set out. Information collected may include:
>
> - National Curriculum levels
>
> - departmental assessments
>
> - reading scores
>
> - advice from pastoral staff
>
> - discussion with staff in the SEN department
>
> - information provided on IEPs
>
> Special Examination arrangements need to be considered not only at Key Stage 3 and 4 but also for internal examinations. How and when these will be discussed should be clarified. Reference to SENCO and examination arrangements from the examination board should be taken into account. Ensuring that staff in the department understand the current legislation and guidance from central government is important, so a reference to the SEN Code of Practice and the levels of SEN intervention is helpful within the policy. Here is a good place also to put a statement about the school behaviour policy and rewards and sanctions, and how the department will make any necessary adjustments to meet the needs of pupils with SEN.

Example

> It is understood that pupils with SEN may receive additional support if they have a statement of SEN, are at School Action Plus or School Action. The staff in the design and technology department will aim to support the pupils to achieve their targets as specified on their IEPs and will provide feedback for IEP or statement reviews. Pupils with SEN will be included in the departmental monitoring system used for all pupils. Additional support will be requested as appropriate.

Resources and learning materials

The department policy needs to specify what differentiated materials are available, where they are kept and how to find new resources. This section could include a statement about working with support staff to develop resources or access specialist resources as needed, and the use of ICT. Teaching strategies may also be identified if appropriate. Advice on more specialist equipment can be sought as necessary, possibly through LEA support services: contact details may be available from the SENCO, or the department may have direct links. Any specially bought subject text or alternative/appropriate courses can be specified as well as any external assessment and examination courses.

Example

> The department will provide suitably differentiated materials and where appropriate, specialist resources for pupils with SEN. Additional texts are available for those pupils working below National Curriculum level 3. At Key Stage 4 an alternative course to GCSE is offered at Entry level but, where possible, pupils with SEN will be encouraged to reach their full potential and follow a GCSE course. Support staff will be provided with curriculum information in advance of lessons and will also be involved in lesson planning. A list of resources is available in the department handbook and on the noticeboard.

Staff qualifications and Continuing Professional Development needs

It is important to recognise and record the qualifications and special skills gained by staff within the department. Training can include not only external courses but also in-house INSET and opportunities such as observing other staff, working to produce materials with other staff, and visiting other establishments. Staff may have hidden skills that might enhance the work of the department and the school, for example some staff might be proficient in the use of sign language.

Example

> A record of training undertaken, specialist skills and training required will be kept in the department handbook. Requests for training will be considered in line with the department and school improvement plan.

Monitoring and reviewing the policy

To be effective any policy needs regular monitoring and review. These can be planned as part of the yearly cycle. The responsibility for the monitoring can rest with the Head of Department but will have more effect if supported by someone from outside acting as a critical friend. This could be the SENCO or a member of the senior management team in school.

Example

> The department SEN policy will be monitored by the Head of Department on a planned annual basis, with advice being sought from the SENCO as part of a three-yearly review process.

Summary

Creating a departmental SEN policy should be a developmental activity to improve the teaching and learning for all pupils but especially for those with special or additional needs. The policy should be a working document that will evolve and change; it is there to challenge current practice and to encourage improvement for both pupils and staff. If departmental staff work together to create the policy, they will have ownership of it; it will have true meaning and be effective in clarifying practice.

CHAPTER 3

Different Types of SEN

This chapter is a starting point for information on the special educational needs most frequently occurring in the mainstream secondary school. It describes the main characteristics of each learning difficulty with practical ideas for use in subject areas, and contacts for further information. Some of the tips are based on good secondary practice while others encourage teachers to try new or less familiar approaches.

The SEN outlined in this chapter are grouped under the headings used in the SEN Code of Practice (DfES 2001):

- cognition and learning

- behavioural, emotional and social development

- communication and interaction

- sensory and/or physical needs

(See Table 2.1 in Chapter 2).

The labels used in this chapter are useful when describing pupils' difficulties but it is important to remember not to use the label in order to define the pupil. Put the pupil before the difficulty, saying 'the pupil with special educational needs' rather than 'the SEN pupil,' 'pupils with MLD' rather than 'MLDs'.

Remember to take care in using labels when talking with parents, pupils or other professionals. Unless a pupil has a firm diagnosis, and parents and pupil understand the implications of that diagnosis, it is more appropriate to describe the features of the special educational need rather than use the label, for example a teacher might describe a pupil's spelling difficulties but not use the term 'dyslexic'.

The number and profile of pupils with special educational needs will vary from school to school, so it is important to consider the pupil with SEN as an individual within your school and subject environment. The strategies contained in this chapter will help teachers adapt that environment to meet the needs of individual pupils within the subject context. For example, rather than saying, 'He can't read the worksheet', recognise that the worksheet is too difficult for the pupil, and adapt the work accordingly. (Example IEPs are included in Appendix 3.1 on the accompanying CD.)

There is a continuum of need within each of the special educational needs listed here. Some pupils will be affected more than others, and show fewer or more of the characteristics described.

The availability and levels of support from professionals within a school (e.g. SENCOs, support teachers, Teaching Assistants) and external professionals (e.g. educational psychologists, Learning Support Service staff, medical staff) will depend on the severity of pupils' SEN. This continuum of need will also impact on the design and technology teacher's planning and allocation of support staff.

Pupils with other, less common, special educational needs may be included in some secondary schools, and additional information on these conditions may be found in a variety of sources. These include the school SENCO, LEA support services, educational psychologists and the Internet.

Asperger's Syndrome

Asperger's Syndrome is a disorder at the able end of the autistic spectrum. People with Asperger's Syndrome have average to high intelligence but share the same Triad of Impairments. They often want to make friends but do not understand the complex rules of social interaction. They have impaired fine and gross motor skills, with writing being a particular problem. Boys are more likely to be affected – with the ratio being 10:1 boys to girls. Because they appear 'odd' and naïve, these pupils are particularly vulnerable to bullying.

Main characteristics

- **Social interaction**

  Pupils with Asperger's Syndrome want friends but have not developed the strategies necessary for making and sustaining friendships. They find it very difficult to learn social norms and to pick up on social cues. Highly social situations, such as lessons, can cause great anxiety.

- **Social communication**

  Pupils have appropriate spoken language but tend to sound formal and pedantic, using little expression and with an unusual tone of voice. They have difficulty using and understanding non-verbal language such as facial expression, gesture, body language and eye-contact. They have a literal understanding of language and do not grasp implied meanings.

- **Social imagination**

  Pupils with Asperger's Syndrome need structured environments, and routines they understand and can anticipate. They excel at learning facts and figures, but have difficulty understanding abstract concepts and in generalising information and skills. They often have all-consuming special interests.

How can the design and technology teacher help?

- Liaise closely with parents, especially over homework.
- Create as calm a classroom environment as possible, particularly during practical lessons.
- Allow the pupil to sit in the same place for each lesson.
- Set up a work buddy system for your lessons.
- Provide additional visual cues in class, for example a step-by-step flow diagram with pictures of how to make the product.
- Give the pupil time to process questions and respond.
- Make sure pupils understand what to do.
- Allow alternatives to writing for recording so that pupils do not spend too many hours on this.
- Use visual timetables and task activity lists.
- Prepare for changes to routines well in advance.
- Give written homework instructions and stick them into an exercise book.
- Have your own class rules and apply them consistently.

The National Autistic Society, 393 City Road, London ECIV 1NG
Tel: 0845 070 4004 Helpline (10 a.m.–4 p.m., Mon–Fri) Tel: 020 7833 2299
Fax: 020 7833 9666
Email: nas@nas.org.uk   Website: http://www.nas.org.uk

Attention Deficit Disorder (with or without hyperactivity) (ADD/ ADHD)

Attention Deficit Hyperactivity Disorder is a term used to describe children who exhibit over-active behaviour and impulsivity and who have difficulty in paying attention. It is caused by a form of brain dysfunction of a genetic nature. ADHD can sometimes be controlled effectively by medication. Children of all levels of ability can have ADHD.

Main characteristics

- difficulty in following instructions and completing tasks
- easily distracted by noise, movement of others, objects attracting attention
- often doesn't listen when spoken to
- fidgets and becomes restless, can't sit still
- interferes with other pupils' work
- can't stop talking, interrupts others, calls out
- runs about when inappropriate
- has difficulty in waiting or taking turns
- acts impulsively without thinking about the consequences

How can the design and technology teacher help?

- Make eye contact and use the pupil's name when speaking to him.
- Keep instructions simple – the one sentence rule.
- Provide clear routines and rules, rehearse them regularly, for example getting ready for practical work, clearing away.
- Sit the pupil away from obvious distractions, e.g. windows, the computer, machinery.
- In busy situations and practical lessons direct the pupil by name to visual or practical objects.
- Encourage the pupil to repeat back instructions before starting a task.
- Tell the pupil when to begin clearly.
- Give two choices – avoid the option of the pupil saying 'No': ' Do you want to use the blue or red acrylic for your holder?'
- Give advance warning when something is about to happen, change or finish with a time, e.g. 'In two minutes I need you (pupil name) to . . .'
- Give specific praise – catch him being good, give attention for positive behaviour.
- Give the pupil responsibilities so that others can see him in a positive light and he develops a positive self-image.

ADD Information Services, PO Box 340, Edgware, Middlesex, HA8 9HL Tel: 020 8906 9068
ADDNET UK www.btinternet.com/~black.ice/addnet/

Autistic Spectrum Disorders (ASD)

The term 'Autistic Spectrum Disorders' is used for a range of disorders affecting the development of social interaction, social communication and social imagination and flexibility of thought. This is known as the 'Triad of Impairments'. Pupils with ASD cover the full range of ability and the severity of the impairment varies widely. Some pupils also have learning disabilities or other difficulties. Four times as many boys as girls are diagnosed with an ASD.

Main characteristics

- **Social interaction**
  Pupils with an ASD find it difficult to understand social behaviour and this affects their ability to interact with children and adults. They do not always understand social contexts. They may experience high levels of stress and anxiety in settings that do not meet their needs or when routines are changed. This can lead to inappropriate behaviour.

- **Social communication**
  Understanding and use of non-verbal and verbal communication is impaired. Pupils with an ASD have difficulty understanding the communication of others and in developing effective communication themselves. They have a literal understanding of language. Many are delayed in learning to speak, and some never develop speech at all.

- **Social imagination and flexibility of thought**
  Pupils with an ASD have difficulty in thinking and behaving flexibly which may result in restricted, obsessional, or repetitive activities. They are often more interested in objects than people, and have intense interests in one particular area such as trains and vacuum cleaners. Pupils work best when they have a routine. Unexpected changes in those routines will cause distress. Some pupils with Autistic Spectrum Disorders have a different perception of sounds, sights, smell, touch, and taste, and this can affect their response to these sensations.

Pupils with an ASD may find D&T particularly difficult because it involves social interaction, social communication and flexibility of thought to complete every design and make project in the practical classroom. However, each case is quite unique and some pupils with an ASD have been known to excel and be gifted in specific areas, for example designing, and observing real products. The teacher must balance allowing the pupil to develop their unique talents and ensuring sufficient development across all areas.

How can the design and technology teacher help?

- Liaise with parents as they will have many useful strategies.

- Provide visual supports in class: objects, pictures, etc.

- Give a symbolic or written timetable for each day.

- Give advance warning of any changes to usual routines.

- Warn pupils when they will need to be flexible and anticipate some distress, for example a food product may take between 10–15 minutes to cook and the pupils may become distressed if it is not ready exactly on time.

- Provide own practical workspace if possible, and allow access to computers for designing.

- Avoid using too much eye contact as it can cause distress.

- Give individual instructions using the pupil's name, e.g. 'Paul, bring me your design folder.'

- Individual projects related to pupil's own interests may be more successful than those set outside their experience requiring them to work as a team.

- Structured projects that guarantee success will build confidence.

- Avoid using metaphor, idiom or sarcasm – say what you mean in simple language.

BEHAVIOURAL, EMOTIONAL AND SOCIAL DEVELOPMENT NEEDS

This term includes behavioural, emotional and social difficulties and Attention Deficit Disorder with or without hyperactivity. These difficulties can be seen across the whole ability range and have a continuum of severity. Pupils with special educational needs in this category are those who have persistent difficulties despite an effective school behaviour policy and a personal and social curriculum.

Behavioural, emotional and social difficulties (BESD)

Main characteristics

- inattentive, poor concentration and lacks interest in school/school work
- easily frustrated, anxious about changes
- unable to work in groups
- unable to work independently, constantly seeking help
- confrontational – verbally aggressive towards pupils and/or adults
- physically aggressive towards pupils and/or adults
- destroys property – their own/others
- appears withdrawn, distressed, unhappy, sulky, may self-harm
- lacks confidence, acts extremely frightened, lacks self-esteem
- finds it difficult to communicate
- finds it difficult to accept praise

How can the design and technology teacher help?

- Check the ability level of the pupil and adapt the level of work to this, support basic skills development such as reading and writing with writing frames, recording pro-formas.
- Consider the pupil's strengths and interests and use them in a design and make assignment.
- Choose a design and make assignment where they are guaranteed success and make a high quality product, for example using CAD/CAM.
- Where a pupil only wants to 'make', choose a task that will only work if some designing is done. Show importance of 'design' in the pupil's favourite products and things of interest to them.
- Tell the pupil what you expect in advance as regards work and behaviour.
- Talk to the pupil to find out a bit about them.
- Position the pupil close to you during practical work, or close to supportive peers.
- Set a target with a reward system, for example have a list of ten tasks that you expect them to complete for the project and tick them off during the lesson.
- Use demonstrations, modelling thinking, step-by-step planners to show pupils what to do next and encourage independence.

- Where pupils produce few/stereotypic ideas because they do not want to risk failure, provide plenty of ideas, alternatives and stimuli.

- Focus your comments on the behaviour, not on the pupil, and offer an alternative way of behaving when correcting the pupil.

- Use positive language and verbal praise whenever possible.

- When a pupil destroys their work, or struggles when they make mistakes, highlight the mistakes and developing ideas of real designers and others. Show how mistakes can be corrected to remove fear of making mistakes.

- If pupils fear judging their work against high achievers when evaluating their own products, make sure it is clear that they are judging against the design specification. Build up supportive peer evaluation.

- Tell the pupil what you want them to do: 'I need you to . . .', 'I want you to . . .', rather than ask. This avoids confrontation and allows for the possibility that there is room for negotiation.

- Give the pupil a choice between two options.

- Stick to what you say.

- Give the pupil responsibilities to increase self-esteem and confidence.

- Plan a 'time out' system. Ask a colleague for help with this.

SEBDA is the new name for the association of workers for children with emotional and behavioural difficulties.
www.awcebd.co.uk

Cerebral palsy (CP)

Cerebral palsy is a persistent disorder of movement and posture. It is caused by damage or lack of development to part of the brain before or during birth or in early childhood. Problems vary from slight clumsiness to more severe lack of control of movements. Pupils with CP may also have learning difficulties. They may use a wheelchair or other mobility aid.

Main characteristics

There are three main forms of cerebral palsy:

- *spasticity* – disordered control of movement associated with stiffened muscles

- *athetosis* – frequent involuntary movements

- *ataxia* – an unsteady gait with balance difficulties and poor spatial awareness

  Pupils may also have communication difficulties.

How can the design and technology teacher help?

- Talk to parents, the physiotherapist – and the pupil.

- Consider the classroom layout and equipment to be used, for example access to workspaces in practical lessons, use of CAD/CAM, adaptions to sewing machines, etc.

- Get the pupil to collect all materials and tools together before they start so that they do not need to fetch things repeatedly.

- Have high academic expectations.

- Use jigs, templates, patterns, pre-cut or pre-made parts if co-ordination and accuracy are issues.

- Use visual supports: objects, pictures, symbols.

- Arrange a work/subject buddy or helper in the class to work under the direction of the pupil.

- Speak directly to the pupil rather than through a Teaching Assistant.

- Ensure access to appropriate IT equipment for the subject – and that it is used, for example word processing.

Scope, PO Box 833, Milton Keynes, MK12 5NY
Tel: 0808 800 3333 (Freephone helpline) Fax: 01908 321051
Email: cphelpline@scope.org.uk Website: http://www.scope.org.uk

Down's Syndrome (DS)

Down's Syndrome is the most common identifiable cause of learning disability. This is a genetic condition caused by the presence of an extra chromosome 21. People with DS have varying degrees of learning difficulties ranging from mild to severe. They have a specific learning profile with characteristic strengths and weaknesses. All share certain physical characteristics but will also inherit family traits in physical features and personality. They may have additional sight, hearing, respiratory, and heart problems.

Main characteristics

- delayed motor skills
- take longer to learn and consolidate new skills
- limited concentration
- difficulties with generalisation, thinking and reasoning
- sequencing difficulties
- stronger visual than aural skills
- better social than academic skills

How can the design and technology teacher help?

- Sit or position the pupil in a practical room where they can best see and hear.
- Speak directly to pupil, reinforce with facial expression, pictures, objects.
- Use simple, familiar language in short sentences.
- Check instructions have been understood.
- Give the pupil time to process information and formulate a response.
- Give the pupil plenty of time to practise basic practical skills and reinforce ones learned earlier.
- Practise sequencing with simple stages of a process – muddled up and placed in order with the pupil.
- Break lessons up into a series of shorter, varied, and achievable tasks.
- Accept other ways of recording: drawings, tape/video recordings, symbols, etc.
- Set differentiated tasks linked to the work of the rest of the class.
- Lead and feed ideas showing finished examples so that the pupil sees the point of designing and making.
- If the ideas developed are impractical and cannot be made by the pupil, explain to them why they might not be able to realise their ideas, but highlight as many positive parts of the ideas as possible.
- Provide age-appropriate resources and activities.
- If the pupil has a limited range of ideas and experience to draw on for design ideas provide a range of age appropriate stimuli and some possible ideas for the pupils to develop.
- Use jigs, templates, patterns, pre-cut or pre-made parts if co-ordination and accuracy are issues.
- Allow working in top groups to give good behaviour models.
- Provide a work buddy.
- Expect unsupported work for part of each lesson.

The Down's Association, 155 Mitcham Road, London SW17 9PG; Tel: 0845 230 0372; Email: info@downs-syndrome.org.uk; Website: http://www.downs-syndrome.org.uk

Fragile X Syndrome

Fragile X Syndrome is caused by a malformation of the X chromosome and is the most common form of inherited learning disability. This intellectual disability varies widely, with up to a third having learning problems ranging from moderate to severe. More boys than girls are affected but both may be carriers.

Main characteristics

- delayed and disordered speech and language development

- difficulties with the social use of language

- articulation and/or fluency difficulties

- verbal skills better developed than reasoning skills

- repetitive or obsessive behaviour such as hand-flapping, chewing, etc.

- clumsiness and fine motor co-ordination problems

- attention deficit and hyperactivity

- easily anxious or overwhelmed in busy environments

How can the design and technology teacher help?

- Liaise with parents.

- Make sure the pupil knows what is to happen in each lesson – visual timetables, work schedules or written lists.

- Ensure the pupil sits or works in practical lessons at the front of the class, in the same seat for all lessons.

- Arrange a work/subject buddy.

- Where possible, keep to routines and give prior warning of all changes.

- Make instructions clear and simple.

- Use visual supports: objects, pictures, symbols.

- Provide checklists and plenty of discussions to help with designing and evaluating products. Help the pupil to evaluate and discuss some favourite products.

- Design directly with the materials.

- Allow the pupil to use a computer to record and access information.

- Give lots of praise and positive feedback.

Fragile X Society, Rood End House, 6 Stortford Road, Dunmow, CM6 1DA
Tel: 01424 813147 (Helpline) Tel: 01371 875100 (Office)
E-mail: info@fragilex.org.uk   Website: http://www.fragilex.org.uk

Moderate learning difficulties (MLD)

The term 'moderate learning difficulties' is used to describe pupils who find it extremely difficult to achieve expected levels of attainment across the curriculum, even with a differentiated and flexible approach. These pupils do not find learning easy and can suffer from low self-esteem and sometimes exhibit unacceptable behaviour as a way of avoiding failure.

Main characteristics

- difficulties with reading, writing and comprehension
- unable to understand and retain basic mathematical skills and concepts
- immature social and emotional skills
- limited vocabulary and communication skills
- short attention span
- under-developed co-ordination skills
- lack of logical reasoning
- inability to transfer and apply skills to different situations
- difficulty remembering what has been taught
- difficulty with organising themselves, following a timetable, remembering books and equipment

How can the design and technology teacher help?

- Check the pupil's strengths, weaknesses and attainment levels.
- Establish a routine within the lesson.
- Keep tasks short and varied.
- Keep listening tasks short or broken up with activities.
- Provide word lists, writing frames, shorten text.
- Try alternative methods of recording information, e.g. drawings, charts, labelling, diagrams, use of ICT.
- Check previously gained knowledge and build on it.
- Repeat information and instructions in different ways.
- Show the child what to do or what the expected outcome is, demonstrate practical skills or show examples of completed work.
- Use practical, concrete, visual examples to illustrate explanations.
- Design directly with the materials.

- Lead and feed ideas showing finished examples so that the pupil sees the point of designing and making.

- If the ideas developed are impractical and cannot be made by the pupil, explain to them why they might not be able to realise their ideas, but highlight as many positive parts of the ideas as possible.

- If the pupil has a limited range of ideas and experience to draw on for design ideas, provide a range of age-appropriate stimuli and some possible ideas for the pupils to develop.

- Use jigs, templates, patterns, pre-cut or pre-made parts if co-ordination and accuracy are issues.

- Question the pupil to check they have grasped a concept or can follow instructions.

- Make sure the pupil always has something to do.

- Use lots of praise, instant rewards, catch them trying hard.

The MLD Alliance, c/o The Elfrida Society, 34 Islington Park Street, London N1 1PX.
www.mldalliance.com/executive.htm

Physical disability (PD)

There is a wide range of physical disabilities, and pupils with PD cover all academic abilities. Some pupils are able to access the curriculum and learn effectively without additional educational provision. They have a disability but do not have a special educational need. For other pupils, the impact on their education may be severe, and the school will need to make adjustments to enable them to access the curriculum.

Some pupils with a physical disability have associated medical conditions which may impact on their mobility. These include cerebral palsy, heart disease, spina bifida and hydrocephalus, and muscular dystrophy. Pupils with physical disabilities may also have sensory impairments, neurological problems, or learning difficulties. They may use a wheelchair and/or additional mobility aids. Some pupils will be mobile but may have significant fine motor difficulties which require support. Others may need augmentative or alternative communication aids.

Pupils with a physical disability may need to miss lessons to attend physiotherapy or medical appointments. They are also likely to become very tired as they expend greater effort to complete everyday tasks. Schools will need to be flexible and sensitive to individual pupil needs.

How can the design and technology teacher help?

- Get to know pupils and parents and they will help you make the right adjustments.
- Maintain high expectations.
- Consider the classroom layout and provision of equipment: plan for provision and access.
- Choose projects carefully, incorporate pupil interests and experiences where possible.
- Provide extra time and, if possible, less complex tasks, or shorter tasks.
- Allow the pupil to leave lessons a few minutes early to avoid busy corridors and give time to get to next lesson.
- Get the pupil to collect all materials and tools together before they start so that they do not need to fetch things repeatedly.
- Set homework earlier in the lesson so instructions are not missed.
- Speak directly to the pupil rather than through a Teaching Assistant.
- Allow a helper to assist under the pupil's instruction, for example a scribe to record designs or a helper for making.
- Use jigs, templates, pre-made parts, CAD/CAM to facilitate making and support accuracy and quality of outcome.
- Let pupils make their own decisions.
- Ensure access to appropriate IT equipment for the lesson – and that it is used!
- Give alternative ways of recording work.
- Plan to cover work missed through medical or physiotherapy appointments.
- Be sensitive to fatigue, especially at the end of the school day.
- Reward all forms of progress.

Semantic Pragmatic Disorder (SPD)

Semantic Pragmatic Disorder is a communication disorder which falls within the autistic spectrum. 'Semantic' refers to the meanings of words and phrases and 'pragmatic' refers to the use of language in a social context. Pupils with this disorder have difficulties understanding the meaning of what people say and in using language to communicate effectively. Pupils with SPD find it difficult to extract the central meaning – saliency – of situations.

Main characteristics

- delayed language development
- fluent speech but may sound stilted or over-formal
- may repeat phrases out of context from videos or adult conversations
- difficulty understanding abstract concepts
- limited or inappropriate use of eye contact, facial expression or gesture
- motor skills problems

How can the design and technology teacher help?

- Get the pupil to sit or work at the front of the room to avoid distractions.
- Use visual supports: objects, pictures, symbols.
- Pair with a work/subject buddy.
- Create a calm working environment with clear rules.
- Be specific and unambiguous when giving instructions.
- Make sure instructions are understood, especially when using subject-specific vocabulary that can have another meaning in a different context, for example 'fold', 'shape', 'saw', 'bend', 'seam', 'flour'.

AFASIC, 2nd Floor, 50–52 Great Sutton Street, London EC1V 0DJ
Tel: 0845 355 5577 (Helpline) (11 a.m. to 2 p.m.) Tel: 020 7490 9410
Fax: 020 7251 2834
Email: info@afasic.org.uk Website: http://www.afasic.org.uk

Sensory impairments

Hearing impairment (HI)

The term 'hearing impairment' is a generic term used to describe all hearing loss. The main types of loss are monaural, conductive, sensory and mixed loss. The degree of hearing loss is described as mild, moderate, severe or profound. Some children rely on lip reading, others will use hearing aids, and a small proportion will have British Sign Language (BSL) as their primary means of communication.

How can the design and technology teacher help?

- Check the degree of loss the pupil has.

- Check the best seating position (e.g. away from the hum of OHP, computers, CNC machines, with good ear to speaker).

- Check that the pupil can see your face for facial expressions and lip reading.

- Provide a list of vocabulary, context and visual clues, especially for new subjects.

- During class discussion allow only one pupil to speak at a time and indicate where the speaker is.

- Check that any aids are working and if there is any other specialist equipment available.

- Make sure the light falls on your face and lips. Do not stand with your back to a window.

- If you use interactive whiteboards, ensure that the beam does not prevent the pupil from seeing your face.

- Ban small talk.

Royal Institute for the Deaf (RNID), 19–23 Featherstone Street, London EC1Y 8SL
Tel: 0808 808 0123
British Deaf Association (BDA), 1–3 Worship Street, London EC2A 2AB
British Association of Teachers of the Deaf (BATOD), The Orchard, Leven,
North Humberside, HU17 5QA
www.batod.org.uk

Visual impairment (VI)

Visual impairment refers to a range of difficulties, including those pupils with monocular vision (vision in one eye), those who are partially sighted and those who are blind. Pupils with visual impairment cover the whole ability range and some pupils may have other SEN.

How can the design and technology teacher help?

- Check the optimum position for the pupil, e.g. for a monocular pupil their good eye should be towards the action.

- Always provide the pupil with his own copy of the text.

- Provide enlarged print copies of written text and instructions.

- Check use of ICT (enlarged icons, talking text, teach keyboard skills).

- Do not stand with your back to the window as this creates a silhouette and makes it harder for the pupil to see you.

- Draw the pupil's attention to displays – which they may not notice.

- Make sure the floor is kept free of clutter.

- Tell the pupil if there is a change to the layout of a space.

- Ask if there is any specialist equipment available – enlarged print dictionaries, lights, talking weighing scales, Wikki Stix® for designing rather than drawing.

- Consider activities that explore the use of other senses, such as taste testing.

Royal National Institute of the Blind, 105 Judd Street, London WC1H 9NE
Tel: 020 7388 1266 Fax: 020 7388 2034 Website: http://www.rnib.org.uk

Multi-sensory impairment

Pupils with multi-sensory impairment have a combination of visual and hearing difficulties. They may also have other additional disabilities that make their situation complex. A pupil with these difficulties is likely to have a high level of individual support.

How can the design and technology teacher help?

- The design and technology teacher will need to liaise with support staff to ascertain the appropriate provision within each subject.

- Consideration will need to be given to alternative means of communication.

- Be prepared to be flexible and to adapt tasks, targets and assessment procedures.

- Lead and feed ideas showing finished examples so that the pupil sees the point of designing and making.

- Design directly with the materials.

- If the ideas developed are impractical and cannot be made by the pupil, explain to them why they might not be able to realise their ideas, but highlight as many positive parts of the ideas as possible.

- Provide age-appropriate resources and activities.

- If the pupil has a limited range of ideas and experience to draw on for design ideas, provide a range of age-appropriate stimuli and some possible ideas for the pupils to develop.

- Use jigs, templates, patterns, pre-cut or pre-made parts if co-ordination and accuracy are issues.

Severe learning difficulties (SLD)

This term covers a wide and varied group of pupils who have significant intellectual or cognitive impairments. Many have communication difficulties and/or sensory impairments, in addition to more general cognitive impairments. They may also have difficulties in mobility, co-ordination and perception. Some pupils may use signs and symbols to support their communication and understanding. Their attainments may be within or below level 1 of the National Curriculum, or in the upper P scale range (P4–P8), for much of their school careers.

How can the design and technology teacher help?

- Liaise with parents.

- Arrange a work/subject buddy.

- Use visual supports: objects, pictures, symbols.

- Learn some signs relevant to the subject.

- Allow the pupil time to process information and formulate responses.

- Set differentiated tasks linked to the work of the rest of the class.

- Lead and feed ideas showing finished examples so that the pupil sees the point of designing and making.

- If the pupil has a limited range of ideas and experience to draw on for design ideas, provide a range of age-appropriate stimuli and some possible ideas for the pupils to develop.

- Design directly with the materials.

- Use jigs, templates, patterns, pre-cut or pre-made parts if co-ordination and accuracy are issues.

- Set achievable targets for each lesson or module of work.

- Accept different recording methods: drawings, audio or video recordings, photographs, etc.

- Give access to computers where appropriate.

- Give a series of short, varied activities within each lesson.

Profound and multiple learning difficulties (PMLD)

Pupils with profound and multiple learning difficulties have complex learning needs. In addition to very severe learning difficulties, pupils have other significant difficulties, such as physical disabilities, sensory impairments or severe medical conditions. Pupils with PMLD require a high level of adult support, both for their learning needs and for their personal care.

They are able to access the curriculum through sensory experiences and stimulation. Some pupils communicate by gesture, eye pointing or symbols, others by very simple language. Their attainments are likely to remain in the early P scale range (P1–P4) throughout their school careers (that is below level 1 of the National Curriculum). The P scales provide small, achievable steps to monitor progress. Some pupils will make no progress or may even regress because of associated medical conditions. For this group, experiences are as important as attainment.

How can the design and technology teacher help?

- Liaise with parents and Support Assistants.

- Consider the classroom layout and equipment provided.

- Identify possible sensory experiences in your lessons.

- Use additional sensory supports: objects, pictures, fragrances, music, movements, food, etc.

- Lead and feed ideas showing finished examples so that the pupil sees the purpose of the task.

- Provide a range of age-appropriate stimuli and some possible ideas for the pupils to develop.

- Use adapted equipment.

- Use jigs, templates, patterns, pre-cut or pre-made parts.

- Design directly with the materials, giving choices from a range appropriate to the pupil.

- Take photographs to record experiences and responses.

- Set up a work/subject buddy rota for the class.

- Identify times when the pupil can work with groups.

MENCAP, 117–123 Golden Lane, London EC1Y 0RT
Tel: 020 7454 0454 website: http://www.mencap.org.uk

SPECIFIC LEARNING DIFFICULTIES (SpLD)

The term 'specific learning difficulties' covers dyslexia, dyscalculia and dyspraxia.

Dyslexia

The term 'dyslexia' is used to describe a learning difficulty associated with words and it can affect a pupil's ability to read, write and/or spell. Research has shown that there is no one definitive definition of dyslexia or one identified cause, and it has a wide range of symptoms. Although found across a whole range of ability levels, the idea that dyslexia presents as a difficulty between expected outcomes and performance is widely held.

Main characteristics:

- The pupil may frequently lose their place while reading, make a lot of errors with the high frequency words, have difficulty reading names and have difficulty blending sounds and segmenting words. Reading requires a great deal of effort and concentration.

- The pupil's written work may seem messy, with crossing outs, similarly shaped letters may be confused, such as b/d/p/q, m/w, n/u, and letters in words may be jumbled, such as tired/tried. Spelling difficulties often persist into adult life and these pupils become reluctant writers.

How can the design and technology teacher help?

- Be aware of the type of difficulty and the pupil's strengths.

- Keep instruction sheets simple when making – use step-by-step flow diagrams with visual clues, such as pictures of each process and one action per step.

- Provide key word sheets and writing frames to support designing, planning, making and evaluating.

- Teach and allow the use of word processing, spell checkers and computer-aided learning packages.

- Provide word lists and photocopies of copying from the board.

- Consider alternative recording methods, e.g. pictures, plans, flow charts, mind maps.

- Allow extra time for tasks, including assessments and examinations.

The British Dyslexia Association
Tel: 0118 966 8271 www.bda-dyslexia.org.uk
Dyslexia Institute
Tel: 07184 222 300 www.dyslexia-inst.org.uk

Dyscalculia

The term 'dyscalculia' is used to describe a difficulty in mathematics. This might be either a marked discrepancy between the pupil's developmental level and general ability on measures of specific maths ability, or a total inability to abstract or consider concepts and numbers.

Main characteristics of dyscalculia

- *In number*, the pupil may have difficulty counting by rote, writing or reading numbers, miss out or reverse numbers, have difficulty with mental maths, and be unable to remember concepts, rules and formulae.

- *In maths based* concepts, the pupil may have difficulty with money, telling the time, with directions, right and left, with sequencing events, or may lose track of turns, e.g. in team games, dance.

How can the design and technology teacher help?

- Provide number/word/rule/formulae lists and photocopies of copying from the board.

- Use weighing scales and measuring equipment that is clear and easy to read. Use simple measuring boards and cards so that the pupil does not have to deal with all markings on rulers.

- Make use of ICT and teach the use of calculators.

- Encourage the use of rough paper for working out.

- Plan the setting out of work with it well spaced on the page.

- Provide practical objects that are age appropriate to aid learning.

- Allow extra time for tasks including assessments and examinations.

Website: www.dyscalculia .co.uk

Dyspraxia

The term 'Dyspraxia' is used to describe an immaturity with the way in which the brain processes information, resulting in messages not being properly transmitted.

Main characteristics of dyspraxia

- difficulty in co-ordinating movements, may appear awkward and clumsy

- difficulty with handwriting and drawing, throwing and catching

- difficulty following sequential events, e.g. multiple instructions

- may misinterpret situations, take things literally

- have limited social skills and become frustrated and irritable

- have some articulation difficulties (see verbal dyspraxia)

How can the design and technology teacher help?

- Be sensitive to the pupil's limitations when co-ordination and dexterity are required in designing and making, and plan tasks to enable success.

- Ask the pupil questions to check his understanding of instructions/tasks.

- Help the pupils to sequence their activities with a step-by-step flow chart.

- Consider the best position for a pupil to watch a demonstration; think about having the pupil on the same side as the teacher.

- Check the pupil's seating position to encourage good presentation (both feet resting on the floor, desk at elbow height and ideally with a sloping surface to work on).

- Using grid paper and grid card will help with drawing and modelling.

- Ready-made templates and guides will speed up work and help accuracy.

- A light box can help trace, copy and draw.

- Consider using modified handles and stands to support equipment.

Website: www.dyspraxiafoundation.org.uk

Speech, language and communication difficulties (SLCD)

Pupils with SLCD have problems understanding what others say and/or making others understand what they say. Their development of speech and language skills may be significantly delayed. Speech and language difficulties are common in young children but most problems are resolved during the primary years. Problems that persist beyond the transfer to secondary school will be more severe. Any problem affecting speech, language and communication will have a significant effect on a pupil's self-esteem, and personal and social relationships. The development of literacy skills is also likely to be affected. Even where pupils learn to decode, they may not understand what they have read. Sign language gives pupils an additional method of communication. Pupils with speech, language and communication difficulties cover the whole range of academic abilities.

Main characteristics

- **Speech difficulties**
  Pupils who have difficulties with expressive language may experience problems in articulation and the production of speech sounds, or in co-ordinating the muscles that control speech. They may have a stammer or some other form of dysfluency.

- **Language/communication difficulties**
  Pupils with receptive language impairments have difficulty understanding the meaning of what others say. They may use words incorrectly with inappropriate grammatical patterns, have a reduced vocabulary, or find it hard to recall words and express ideas. Some pupils will also have difficulty using and understanding eye-contact, facial expression, gesture and body language.

How can the design and technology teacher help?

- Talk to parents, speech therapist – and the pupil.
- Learn the most common signs for your subject.
- Use visual supports: objects, pictures, symbols.
- Use the pupil's name when addressing them.
- Give one instruction at a time, using short, simple sentences.
- Give time to respond before repeating a question.
- Make sure pupils understand what they have to do before starting a task.
- Provide alternatives for communication, for example a scribe to record designs and views about products.
- Design directly with the materials, giving pupil choices.
- Pair with a work/subject buddy.
- Give access to a computer or other IT equipment appropriate to the subject.
- Give written homework instructions.

ICAN, 4 Dyer's Buildings, Holborn, London EC1N 2QP; Tel: 0845 225 4071;
Email: info@ican.org.uk   website: http://www.ican.org.uk
AFASIC, 2nd Floor, 50–52 Great Sutton Street, London EC1V 0DJ
Tel: 0845 355 5577 (Helpline) Tel: 020 7490 9410 Fax: 020 7251 2834
Email: info@afasic.org.uk   website: http://www.afasic.org.uk

Tourette's Syndrome (TS)

Tourette's Syndrome is a neurological disorder characterised by tics. Tics are involuntary, rapid or sudden movements or sounds that are frequently repeated. There is a wide range of severity of the condition with some people having no need to seek medical help while others have a socially disabling condition. The tics can be suppressed for a short time but will be more noticeable when the pupil is anxious or excited.

Main characteristics

Physical tics

These range from simple blinking or nodding, through more complex movements, to more extreme conditions such as echopraxia (imitating actions seen) or copropraxia (repeatedly making obscene gestures).

Vocal tics

Vocal tics may be as simple as throat clearing or coughing, but can progress to be as extreme as echolalia (the repetition of what was last heard) or coprolalia (the repetition of obscene words).

Tourette's Syndrome itself causes no behavioural or educational problems but other, associated, disorders such as Attention Deficit Hyperactivity Disorder (ADHD) or Obsessive Compulsive Disorder (OCD) may be present .

How can the design and technology teacher help?

- Establish a rapport with the pupil.

- Talk to the parents.

- Agree an 'escape route' signal should the tics become disruptive.

- Allow the pupil to work at the back of the room to prevent staring.

- Give access to a computer to reduce handwriting.

- Design directly with the materials.

- Make sure the pupil is not teased or bullied.

- Be alert for signs of anxiety or depression.

Tourette Syndrome (UK) Association
PO Box 26149, Dunfermline, KY12 7YU
Tel: 0845 458 1252 (Helpline) Tel: 01383 629600 (Admin.) Fax: 01383 629609
Email: enquiries@tsa.org.uk   Website: http://www.tsa.org.uk

Appendix 3.2 on the CD which accompanies this book provides an activity which is designed to help staff remember strategies to help children with some of the more common SEN.

The Inclusive Design and Technology Classroom

The value of design and technology for pupils with SEN

Design and technology can be a very popular and valuable subject for pupils with special educational needs because the practical nature of the learning experiences make it accessible to pupils of all abilities. They draw on knowledge and understanding from across the curriculum, develop their numeracy, literacy and communication skills, and are required to apply these in practical ways. This may consolidate skills from other lessons and reinforce learning with positive outcomes. Designing and making usable products can give pupils a real sense of achievement as they can benefit from seeing their own progress and taking responsibility for their own learning. Their personal engagement with the task often improves attention span, patience, persistence and commitment so that, despite their special needs, pupils can achieve results that stand comparison with, and occasionally even outshine, their peers. Design and technology offers them the chance to experience achievement at a level that may seldom occur elsewhere in their school life.

Design and technology provides particular opportunities for:

- practical learning experiences which promote success and raise achievement

- focusing on real scenarios and design problems that are meaningful to pupils

- using appropriate and differentiated materials to suit pupils of differing abilities, enabling access to the curriculum for all

- communicating using a range of methods – avoiding over-reliance on the written word

- using ICT as a means to pupils realising, developing and enhancing their work

- access to and supporting learning in other subjects, e.g. maths and science

- work on personally motivated design tasks where the pupil takes ownership of their work and of their own learning

- working within a flexible range of contexts and topics that can be adapted to suit individual interests and motivations

- pupils to work at their own pace and level with appropriate teacher support and intervention

- individually negotiated targets between the teacher and pupil that can be reviewed as required – those pupils who need to work at a slower pace can do so, and pupils who work more quickly can be further challenged to develop their work with activities which extend and enrich their experience

Planning within D&T

Effective planning takes account of the different abilities and interests of each pupil and should enable all of them to progress and demonstrate their achievements. The most effective way to secure success is to think positively and create learning opportunities appropriate to each pupil's needs rather than concentrating on identifying difficulties.

Your role as a D&T teacher

Individual Education Plans (IEPs) should specify how the curriculum will be adapted to take account of the particular learning difficulty. For further information on IEPs see Chapter 6.

Adaptations might include:

- changes to the type of task

- special support given to carry out the activities

- modified learning resources

The examples given in this publication show how units can be adapted to change the type of task or give special support and modified resources.

Considering special educational needs involves teachers in:

- taking account of the difficulties which pupils may encounter in the learning process

- identifying the impact this may have on pupils' development

- developing appropriate strategies for supporting pupils with these difficulties

---

LONG AND MEDIUM-TERM PLANNING

Use the following checklist to help with long and medium-term curriculum planning in your department or faculty:

1. List the learning difficulties of pupils.
2. Indicate any statemented pupils and the nature of their special provision. Include health and safety implications and medical procedures.
3. Outline any support-teacher time available.
4. Outline responsibilities of support-teacher.
5. List any learning support resources available, including local centres or organisations.
6. Indicate how provision for SEN is incorporated into schemes of work and project planning.
7. Identify any specialist SEN INSET for individual D&T teachers.
8. List any targeted funding for SEN support for D&T.
9. Indicate methods of recording attainments and outline any special provision in relation to exams and tests.

(The prompt sheets in Appendices 4.1 and 4.2 on the CD which accompanies this book – 'Short-term planning checklist' and 'Planning for differentiation' – may help you.)

Planning inclusive design and make assignments, focused practical tasks and product evaluation activities

Design and Make assignments

Designing and making assignments (DMAs) involve a complex interplay between:

- exploring and clarifying the task

- generating, developing and communicating ideas and proposals

- testing, evaluating and modifying

- planning and making

It is this interplay that makes design and technology particularly demanding for pupils. It is not possible for a pupil to be developing capability if the activity is reduced to a linear teacher-controlled craft activity, where the designing and the outcome is prescribed step by step.

In relation to these processes, pupils will have particular strengths in certain types of work. It is possible to devise activities for some pupils based on their strengths and successes. This may mean centring D&T activities around 'making' and letting other important processes be incorporated through and around making, for example using three-dimensional 'mock-ups' rather than drawings. The interplay of designing and making can, therefore, also be a strength as well as a demand for these pupils, where designing is always considered in close relation to making.

DMAs provide pupils with the chance to put their knowledge and skills to the test to meet challenges that address real needs and wants. These assignments also enable pupils to develop their confidence and ability to apply design ideas and concepts in concrete, practical ways. They will have opportunities to work as individuals or in a team, learning from the work of others. Designing and making assignments should be planned flexibly so that adequate differentiation is possible. All pupils should experience the whole designing and making process, but some pupils will complete some aspects in more depth or in a more complex way (enrichment activities), and a few will complete additional tasks (extension activities), where this is appropriate for them.

Pupils often find it easier to work on shorter, more focused assignments rather than longer, open tasks. Shorter tasks provide small elements of success, rewarding and motivating the pupil regularly – the accumulation of success and achievement can be structured to ensure progression:

- Use contexts that pupils are familiar with.

- Adapt or make improvements, or add a new feature to the design of a product rather than 'invent' a whole new product where their experience is limited.

- Design a product where they are given guidance toward alternative solutions. However, it is important to avoid tokenism – there ought to be an opportunity for real designing, real decision taking.

- Manage a project where certain aspects are restricted (for example, the size and shape of a box), but there are still significant opportunities for designing and for independent work (for example, designing the puzzle to put in the box, decorating the outside of the box).

- Join in a project part way through, for example where the researching has been completed so they can get into the modelling and making aspects more quickly.

Some examples

- *Snacks – pasty filling* task requires the pupils to design a new filling only, rather than the whole pasty, or an even more open task of snack food development.

- *Disk case/wallet* requires the pupils to design a case for their own personal use and this will be a context that is familiar to the pupil so makes research requirements real but limited.

Focused practical tasks

Focused practical tasks (FPTs) enable teachers to ensure that pupils practise particular skills and knowledge, consolidating these as they are acquired. They are closely structured and teacher led so that pupils practise or learn a skill or process. They build pupils' confidence and give them ideas for their design. These 'mini-making' activities are highly motivating for pupils as they can see the results of their progress and efforts immediately. For example, a teacher may organise a series of biscuit-making activities before the pupils consider how to design and make a new biscuit product. Teachers should use short, focused tasks to provide particular emphases, providing opportunity for pupils to achieve success in one or more D&T processes.

Pupils will find it easier to:

- repeat and reinforce previously learned skills and processes on a regular basis

- follow a simplified set of instructions with clear pictures and diagrams independently

- absorb a small amount of information or a few instructions at one time, breaking down the process into smaller stages where possible

- plan their own work if they have practised this (e.g. putting muddled sets of instructions in the right order) (See Time planner support sheet in Appendix 4.3 on the CD which accompanies this book.)

- spell and recognise the names of important pieces of equipment and processes (e.g. using key word sheets or posters to help them). (See Appendix 4.4 'Key words' on the CD which accompanies this book. Ingredient words, action words, equipment words and material words are given.)

Some examples

- *Snacks – pasty filling* – making a pasty from a set recipe to practise the process and understand how the product behaves

- *Chocolate novelties* – practising using a vacuum former

- *Disk case/wallet* – learning how to make different seams

- *Colouring textiles* – learning how to tie-dye and batik

- *Sheet material* – making a paper clock in card to practise 3D modelling

Product evaluation activities

These are activities through which pupils can investigate, disassemble and evaluate products, providing the opportunity to build knowledge, skills and understanding that can be used to inform other D&T activities. Pupils can be encouraged to evaluate other designers' work against clear criteria and through discussion.

Pupils will find it easier to

- look at a limited range of products at one time

- have a mixture of familiar products and less familiar ones to look at

- use proforma worksheets to record their responses

- discuss, examine and taste products as a group rather than relying on written accounts

Some examples

- *Snacks – pasty filling* – taking apart and tasting pasty-like products or looking at labels to get ideas for their designs

- *Feeding special groups* – evaluating some vegetarian products that are available

- *Chocolate novelties* – examining chocolate-shaped products that you can buy and working out how they have been made

- *Sheet material* – looking at products made from sheet materials and how they have been made

Supporting designing and making

> Most pupils with special educational needs cope well with the making aspects of work and teachers are effective in providing appropriate guidance. There is less effective support in the initial design work and in ensuring that written information is accessible to all pupils who have reading or language difficulties. (Ofsted (1995): *D&T, a Review of Inspection Findings 1994/1995*)

Ofsted reports comment every year that 'making' aspects are better taught than 'designing' at Key Stage 3, and the *National Strategy KS3 Foundations Subjects D&T National Dissemination 2004–5* will focus on helping teachers address this area.

As pupils with SEN require even more support in this part of D&T, particular attention should be paid to planning how pupils can access and be successful in their initial design work, for example supporting the recording of ideas quickly; encouraging modelling with materials rather than drawing ideas; providing stimulus for ideas; accessing and applying simple research information and presenting and evaluating ideas. (See Appendices 4.5 and 4.6 on the CD which accompanies this book for example support sheets, 'Design Sheet', 'Design Ideas Planner 1' and 'Design Ideas Planner 2'.)

The National Association of Advisers and Inspectors for Design and Technology (NAAIDT) stated in 1995:

> Designing presents intellectual challenges which are not yet fully explored with respect to pupils with special needs nor do we understand fully how

these challenges differ from, for instance, language development, reading or numeracy

Diversity in approaches to designing should be valued and teachers should be aware of adopting too rigid an approach to the way pupils are asked to record and communicate their design ideas and developments.

For activity focused on the 'making' part of the Programme of Study, it is assumed that the teacher will often give one-to-one support. However, particular attention should be paid to facilitate independent making, for example: key words sheets; flow charts to help with the order of making; and simplified, visual instruction sheets which explain a process step-by-step.

SUPPORTING DESIGNING

Identify a current group who are working on a designing and making assignment.

1) What special challenges to the pupils are there during the designing stages of the project?
2) What strategies have you used successfully to help pupils during the designing stages?

Teachers often report the following difficulties during designing:

1. Clumsiness or difficulties in expressing ideas and in producing drawings

2. Difficulties in recording thoughts and communicating information

3. A limited range of ideas and experiences

4. Difficulty in relating needs and concepts of task to ideas and solutions

5. Frustration and failure caused by restricted methods of communication imposed – too much written work expected

6. Pupil unable to connect designing with making

7. Pupil only wants to make something and not design/draw ideas

8. Lack of confidence limits ideas: pupil often copies familiar products and plays safe, and quickly becomes disheartened when they see others' design ideas

9. Lack of pride in work

10. Ideas too narrow or stereotypical

11. Ideas are unrealistic, impractical and beyond the pupil's making ability

12. Pupil finds it difficult to sustain momentum on a long project: not interested in detail or accuracy, simply wants to get the project finished quickly

13. Lacks patience, does not want to revisit a task or improve work, sees little value in testing and evaluating

14. Afraid of judging own work against peers or others

15. Pupil easily loses confidence in work

Suggested approaches

For example, for a pupil who:

- finds working ideas on paper too abstract – and cannot relate to the materials or processes

- wants to get on and make the product

- lacks confidence to present ideas to others

The following strategies could be used:

- hands-on activities to encourage more than writing and graphical presentation of ideas

- starting points for *drawing ideas* should be replaced with structured questioning, moving to exploring and trying out ideas with 3D materials. (See Appendix 4.7 on the accompanying CD for an example of a planned sequence of questions and Appendix 4.8 for a plenary case study)

- building confidence in presenting ideas by starting as a group rather than as an individual

- teachers modelling thinking for the pupils – explaining a designing decision-making process aloud for pupils, for example when making a fruit kebab (see Appendix 4.9 on the accompanying CD for an example of modelling thinking)

Ideas for supporting designing in a number of different projects

- *Snacks – pasty filling* – a recipe can be given for pupils to make as a prototype model. With the knowledge of how ingredients behave and interact, they are then able to suggest adaptations and add their own variations and ideas.

- *Feeding special groups* – the computer can be used for nutritional modelling to compare different recipes before they are made. This saves complex calculations, and results can be shown visually as bar charts.

- *Chocolate novelties* – the form of the chocolate can be sketched (on paper or using a computer) or made in scrap paper or card before making the form or mould.

- *Disk case/Wallet* – paper mock-ups or scrap fabric can be used to design the disk case and work through different ideas.

- *Colouring textiles* – a template for the product (T-shirt) can be provided (on paper or computer) and pupils can model their ideas with swatches of sample fabrics, paper cuttings and sketches.

- *Sheet material* – thumbnail models can be made in card to explore ideas and develop them further: bending and shaping card, exploring sheet materials' limitations.

Strategies for keeping pupils motivated and improving pupil outcomes

Some of the following may seem obvious to experienced teachers. Even so, perhaps you will find some new ideas and that this checklist is useful to you.

- Ensure that their learning objectives are clear for pupils and expressed in accessible language.

- Avoid abstract contexts: over a key stage provide a range of concrete starting points, materials and techniques as some will be of more interest to some pupils than others. Encourage pupils to work on tasks related to their hobbies, interests and strengths.

- Choose projects where pupils are able to produce good quality products, where success is guaranteed and they will be proud of what they have designed and made. This will help their confidence and self-esteem, so that they are able to take risks later with their designing and making.

- There is a fine line between teacher intervention and taking over the pupil's project. The pupil's experience should not solely be one where they are following a designing and making process step-by-step with the teacher doing most of the thinking.

- Ensure that targets match individual's abilities and are challenging but achievable – this will promote self-esteem. The response to 'Am I asking too much?' needs to be 'No, but I am asking a lot!' Provide clear and achievable next steps towards improvement.

- Keep projects short and give regular feedback. Consider the length and complexity of tasks presented: some pupils may be daunted by length, or what they see as a difficult task, and lack the confidence to get started.

- Provide a supportive structure and show pupils a manageable way through the task. Break up the activity into smaller tasks with specific targets – use a tick list or wallchart so that pupils are clear about what they are working towards and where they are in relation to the completion of the project. A project can be broken into smaller steps without being overly prescriptive:

instead of broad stages such as 'research' a list of sub-stages could be given such as:

1. Write five questions for your survey.
2. Ask your target audience to answer your survey.
3. Record your results.
4. Present your results.
5. Discuss your results with your teacher.

This is motivating where pupils have the opportunity to achieve at least one or two targets each lesson and keep up the pace. They can be encouraged to tick them off as they achieve each one. Lists of targets can be divided into essential (everyone must do these) and extension (you can chose to do these if you want to, or have time).

- Provide lots of stimulus for the project, including a number of design solutions; use visits as a stimulus for design contexts and invite experts into the classroom to work alongside pupils (make sure they are well briefed).

- Use rewards, such as an end-of-project certificate that can be presented in assembly. Use classroom rewards systems such as merit marks, stickers and stamps or personal comments on achievement in folders. (See Appendix 4.10 on the accompanying CD for an example of a project certificate.)

- Reduce the amount of reading, researching and written recording required. Allow for a greater diversity of learning styles. Give pupils the opportunity to clarify their ideas through discussion rather than relying on writing.

- Pupils who have language difficulties, or experience difficulties in expressing ideas, may be helped by key words (posters or worksheets or labels around the room), flow diagrams and time plans, good use of simple questions, use of worksheets or design prompts with helpful graphics.

- For pupils with literacy difficulties, the use of modelling, role play, tape recorders, video and photographs for recording should be explored to help them to communicate, develop and record their ideas, as well as to interact with a range of communications technologies.

- Difficulties with planning can be helped by pupils being shown good examples of how others have planned (e.g. other pupils or professional designers) so that they can see what good planning entails, or by giving them practice in 'planning retrospectively' before they go on to forward plan. Pupils often find it easier to give an account of what they have done, rather than what they intend to do. Alternatively, they can be given planning sheets to complete, or part complete, or stages to put in the right order to provide a structure for their thinking. Of course, teacher demonstrations can also help – to show children how to order their work and develop spatial relationships.

- For those who only remember a limited number of instructions and have difficulties listening – avoid long introductions at the beginning of lessons and long lists of instructions. Ensure that the pupils have an overview of the whole task and then structure a task so that a limited number of instructions are given, and these are carried out before the pupil is given more instructions. Increase the range of sources for the instructions: from worksheets, computer, teacher, wall charts, etc. If on a continuing project, at the end of the lesson encourage pupils to list what they will do when they come to you next. You can then check this list and add personalised details to it in readiness for the next lesson so the pupils will be able to restart work immediately without waiting for instructions.

- Provide varied examples of successful presentation. Display pupils' work regularly around the school. Encourage the use of word processing and computer-aided design to enhance presentation.

- Allow opportunities for some pupils to have extra time to work on their project, perhaps during lunchtime or after school.

- Consider the use of computer-aided manufacture, specially adapted tools and equipment, templates, jigs and patterns and other shortcuts to aid completion of making tasks.

Practical resources to help pupils with SEN

General resources

A tape or audio/video recorder
Record the pupil's design ideas, comments, plans and evaluations using an audio recorder. For some pupils this enables them to express their designing and making in ways that writing or drawing might not.

A teacher can also record the main stages of a process so that the pupils can play it back and use it at their own pace. For example, a school records instructions about how to thread a sewing machine onto CD and the pupils listen to this through a personal player with headphones as they set up the machines if they cannot remember how to do it.

A concept keyboard/ tablet PC/touch-sensitive screen
A touch-sensitive electronic panel can be linked to the computer to provide some pupils with an input facility other than a qwerty keyboard. Overlay panels or sheets can be placed onto the concept keyboard to provide symbols or words which, when touched, trigger signals on the keyboard, and thus to the computer. For example, pictures of ingredients and equipment for a design can be chosen in this way, or words for an evaluation can be given. Plastic key panels are also available to fit directly over the keyboard to simplify and enlarge the range and uses of keys.

Colour overlays
Some pupils find colour-tinted plastic overlay sheets help them to read and remember certain words. They could be used to highlight particular words or instructions.

Organising practical rooms

Organising the equipment in the classroom

Large lower-case name labels or Braille labels/ symbols and digital photos should be used on equipment cupboards and areas. This will assist all pupils greatly in working independently and organising themselves. They learn the names of the equipment and where they are kept.

Avoid storing regularly used items in places that are difficult to reach, such as the back of cupboards, at the top of wall units or in low cupboards. Use carousels and pull-out or pull-down drawers to improve access to places that are difficult to reach.

Organising materials and equipment at the start of a practical

To conserve energy, get the pupil to collect together all materials and tools before they start. They may also then get greater benefit from a perching stool because they will not need to get up repeatedly to fetch the things they need.

Organising demonstrations

Consider the best position for a pupil to watch a demonstration. It is easy to forget that many of the children are seeing the process you are demonstrating from an upside-down position. Think about having pupils on the same side as the teacher if that will help. Sometimes the use of a mirror for left-handed pupils helps them, for example watching the mirror instead of the teacher when learning how to sew or thread a needle.

Storyboards/key word sheets/planners

Visual reminders and step-by-step explanations of processes will be very helpful to all pupils, for example a recipe or instruction sheet for making a product. Digital cameras can be used to take photos of the main stages, with key words added for reference.

Safety tips

- Low temperature electric glue guns are safer than other glue guns and can provide a quick-joint facility.

- A sewing machine needle guard designed to protect the needle during transportation can be used to reduce the hazards of machine use with some pupils.

- A safe-cut electric modelling saw which relies on vibrating rather than a rotating or sliding blade can be used for cutting out curved profiles and templates.

- Low voltage or rechargeable power tools cut down the number of trailing leads and the risk of electrical injuries.

- A roller, wheel or rotary guillotine can be used to cut paper, card and plastic and may be safer for some pupils than scissors.

D&T specific tools and adaptions

Use computer-aided manufacturing and processing to improve the quality of the outcomes if appropriate, for example computerised embroidery for sewing logos and letters automatically, plotter cutters to produce iron-on motifs and graphics, milling machines and routers for producing complex shaped pieces, bread maker for mixing and kneading bread. For more information, see www.cadinschools.org.uk

The Ellison Letter Machine

This is a simple lever-operated press tool with a wide selection of very accurate press knife tools. The machine cuts out precision shapes, including nets, lettering, finger puppets and a massive selection of novelty shapes. The press knives will cut a variety of materials, including card, felt, foam, vinyl, etc. This is an excellent tool for use in developing graphic products as it provides the opportunity to print or hand decorate and to combine different elements, and can be used in collaboration with computer printouts to produce very high quality products.

In addition to the variety of products the machine can make, it is also an excellent introduction to industrial style production at Key Stage 3 or 4. Batch production is very easy to organise and, because the machine is so portable, it can be attached to a variety of surfaces to allow maximum flexibility.

The Roland PNC960 Camm1

This is a high quality plotter cutter for use with computers. It can be fitted with a pen to allow line drawings to be produced, or fitted with a knife for cutting self-adhesive vinyl, card nets, cardboard engineering, or even self-adhesive wood veneers. Amongst the applications is the production of graphics to be stuck onto products, silk screen masks for printing, iron-on vinyl for customising garments, etc.

The Roland Stika

This is a small scanning and cutting device which can be used free-standing or linked to a computer. Even simple hand-drawn images can be turned into self-adhesive vinyl within minutes.

The Poem Embroidery Machine

This is a computerised embroidery system. It has a lot of scope for personalising fabric products.

The Workcentre

This provides a range of manufacturing processes in one table-top unit. A range of jigs and fixtures allows pupils to cut, drill and bend resistant materials accurately and with the least amount of effort.

The Badgemaker

This is a table-top machine which can be used to produce a range of products based around the button badge idea. It is excellent for production line work. There is also a foot-operated model available.

The Metalcraft System

This is a range of small-scale metal working tools for cutting, bending, scrolling punching and riveting. They are excellent for full-scale batch production or one-off crafted items. A range of accessories provides the finishing touches to small or large-scale constructions.

Braille and large print rulers, measuring equipment

Specialist equipment suppliers for those with visual impairments will have a range of measuring devices. Choose weighing scales that are easy to read for all pupils, with clearly marked measures, for example digital scales. Talking weighing scales are also useful.

Simple measures (using cups or spoonfuls) can be used for some recipes. Use simple cooker timers that can be set easily to remind pupils of cooking time.

Simple measuring boards or cards can be made to help all pupils mark and measure sizes into materials, without having to deal with all the markings on a ruler. For example, a stepped board can be made with standard or required sizes for the project – clearly marked with sizes and colour coded. When the pupil uses it, the measure is placed on the material and length required marked off. Pupils can quickly see the size and remember the colour more easily.

Grid paper/grid-printed card

Grid paper with lines at different angles can help pupils draw in 3D. Grid card is helpful for modelling.

Templates and guides

Ready-made templates and guides will speed up work and help with accuracy, ensuring a better quality result.

Light boxes

The upward shining light can help to trace, copy and draw.

Adapted kitchen equipment

Use appropriate adapted equipment to assist pupils. There is a wide range available, for example carrying trays, kettle tipping devices, kettles that change colour to indicate they have boiled, accessible ovens and grills, easy-to-operate can openers, jar stabilisers, cool wall toasters, serrated edged knives rather than smooth edged knives, different handled and shaped peelers, etc. You can get advice from your local disabled living centre www.dlcc.org.uk. They may be able to help you access second-hand equipment.

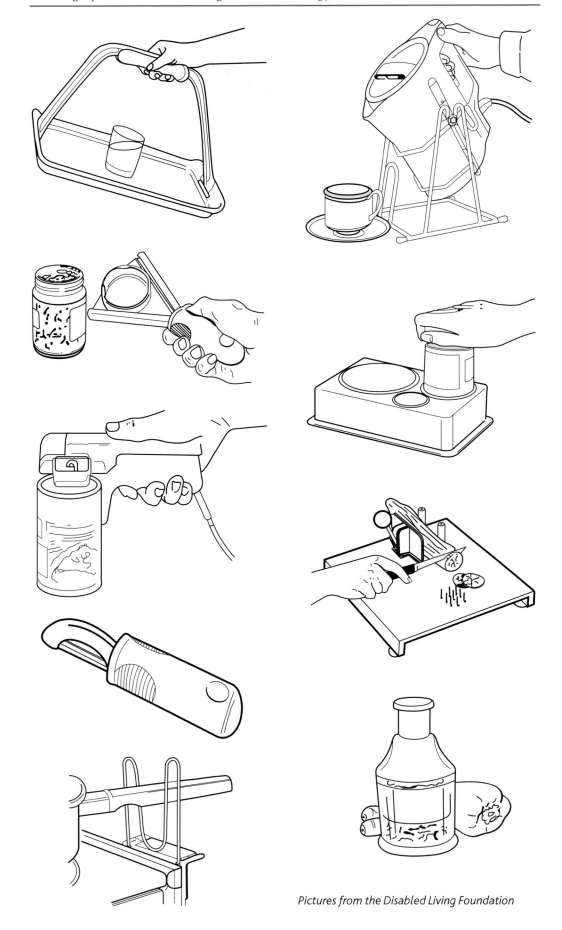

Pictures from the Disabled Living Foundation

Sticky pads and tape

Use sticky tape, pads or rubber feet to hold things, such as a piece of cuttlefish bone while carving out a mould (see jewellery project Chapter 5). This helps pupils who do not have the strength, co-ordination or manual control to hold something still with one hand and perform an operation or process with the other hand.

Hand-drill stands

Use a stand or holding jig to clamp the drill in a vertical position, thereby releasing the hands to assist drilling and removing some of the complexity. Using a hand drill is quite difficult as there are five or six physical and mental actions involved.

Mixing bowls

Blending together ingredients by hand can be a particular problem if pupils have a weak grip or the use of one hand only. A slip-resistant mat could be used under the mixing bowl to help hold it in place while they are mixing. This should work well if the contents being stirred are of a fairly loose consistency. If pupils are trying to blend together stiffer ingredients, use a bowl with a suction base or a bowl holder. Some specially designed kitchen units have pull-out boards with a circular cut-out for this purpose. If a pupil finds this task particularly difficult, consider using a powered whisk or blender.

Electric mixers

Make use of equipment with stands such as an electric mixer with a bowl that is held, rather than a hand-held beater. Choose one that has:

- a clear plastic bowl so that you can observe the food within

- a handle on the bowl for easier handling

- attachments which can be easily handled and positioned

- controls that are within easy view and not recessed

Microwave ovens

Microwave and combination ovens have several advantages over conventional ovens:

- They are compact and can be more easily sited at a convenient height.

- They are versatile and can be used to cook a variety of different foods.

- They cook more quickly and are therefore more economical to use.

- It is easier to cook small quantities of food.

- Less liquid is needed for the cooking process.

- Plastic containers can be used which are lighter and do not conduct heat.

Saucepans

A second hand-hold, particularly on larger saucepans, will help with lifting and positioning the pan. Most lids have knob-shaped handles which can be difficult to grasp. D-shaped handles are easier and can be lifted with the handle of a kitchen utensil. Some pupils may not be able to lift a pan of hot water easily and safely. If the hob is level with the adjacent work surface they should be encouraged to slide the saucepan off the heat. Use a wire basket insert to cook vegetables in. This can be lifted out of the pan when the vegetables are cooked, making straining easier. The water in the saucepan can be left to cool down before it is tipped away. A pan handle holder can be used to stabilise a saucepan if a pupil has the use of one hand only and needs to stir its contents, or just needs some extra help. (See picture in section on adapted kitchen equipment.)

Modifying handles and grips

Choose equipment with larger handles or modify handles for pupils who experience difficulty in gripping, holding and manipulating equipment. One temporary adaptation is to place a slit tennis ball over the problematic handle. Polymorph can be used to quickly make made-to-measure grips for individual hands.

Using an extra hand when using scissors, snips and cutters

Clamp or fix one of the handles of the scissors etc. into a vice and clamp or fix to the edge of the work table. This leaves just one handle to operate; co-ordination and accuracy improve quickly and the downward pressure on the one free handle increases cutting efficiency. *Remove the tool from vice when not in use.*

Chopping boards

Some pupils may find it easier to use a chopping device rather than a knife – as the handle is pushed down, the blades cut the food inside.

A slip-resistant mat placed under a chopping board will help to hold it in place, or some boards are supplied with slip-resistant feet or suction cups on their underside. Some boards also include spikes to stabilise food.

If pupils need to slice a loaf, there are bread guides that will help them to cut even slices, particularly useful if they have a visual impairment.

Also useful if a pupil is partially sighted, is a coloured board to contrast with the food they are preparing, or a board that has a different coloured perimeter.

Some chopping boards have fold-up sides making a shunt to assist with transferring chopped food into a saucepan or peelings into the bin. An integral handle can help pupils to position and carry the board.

Electrical equipment

Use plugs that are easy to remove from the socket.

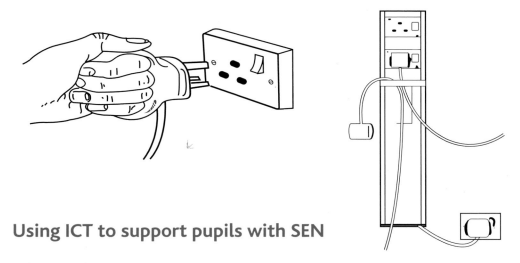

Using ICT to support pupils with SEN

There are several ways in which ICT can have a valuable role in relation to D&T for pupils with SEN. One way is as a support for communicating (such as 'writing with symbols'), another is an aid for modelling ideas (such as graphics and CAD software, or spreadsheets), and another is in making activities using computer-aided manufacturing (CAM) equipment such as embroidery machines, plotter/cutters, etc. One of the benefits of using ICT is that the quality of the product can be greatly enhanced as the pupils are not limited by their motor skills or held back by their difficulties in presenting their ideas in design drawings, or have to rely on the teacher for oral instructions. Pupils with SEN should have high expectations; they are surrounded by high quality images and products and become highly motivated when they realise that using ICT means that they can produce 'professional' looking designs and products. Often, using ICT means that they are released from the constraints that hold them back and are allowed access to a whole new designing and making world.

Research

CD-ROMs and other reference software can facilitate research and allow pupils to access material through multimedia. The visual presentation of information and facilities such as text-to-speech utilities can give access to those with reading difficulties.

Presentation

Information can be presented in a number of formats: text, graphics, animation, digitised images, recorded sound, multimedia, etc.

Subject-specific software

Programs exist to support pupils at a wide variety of levels. These include design, simulation and modelling programs and those which deal with nutritional analysis. These programs offer immediate feedback and allow pupils to present their work in a stimulating and interesting way.

Specialised ICT resources

Supported word-processing

- *Speech feedback* – Talking word-processors allow pupils to review their work and help with writing up research and evaluations.

- *Prediction* – By offering options to complete words, pupils are encouraged to use a more extensive vocabulary and to attempt 'difficult' spellings. Many pupils recognise words that they cannot spell from scratch. Combining prediction with speech feedback offers a great deal of support which can be further enhanced by the use of subject-specific dictionaries.

- *On-screen grids* – Programs such as *Clicker* allow pupils to access information in a multimedia form. They can act as word lists but also have facilities to incorporate sound, graphics and video. Switch access can be used for those who have a keyboard or mouse.

Symbols

Symbols can aid understanding and communication of ideas. Instructions can have symbols attached and 'Writing with Symbols' is a word processor that attaches graphics to the text. This means that pupils can have talking instructions such as recipes or methods of producing an item developed by the teacher. This is very useful but a computer needs to be accessible near to where pupils are working. This has advantages over tape-recorded material as the visual clues provide extra help and give prompts for quicker access.

Other programs to support learners with special educational needs

Clicker4 – Crick Computing (Acorn, Mac, PC) John Crick
Multimedia tool that can act as a talking, on-screen word list with graphics to aid understanding. Can be put to a variety of other uses, including sequencing, matching, multimedia presentations, talking books, explorations of on-screen environments, quizzes and other games to assist learning. Switch versions available including grids to access *Penfriend* on the Acorn version (see below).

Switch Access For Windows (SAW) – ACE Centre (PC)
Access to the computer for those unable to use a keyboard or mouse. Grids to give access to many common programs, including *Prophet* (see below), as well as a designer version to make your own grids.

Penfriend – Design Concepts (Acorn), *Prophet* – ACE Centre (PC), *Co:Writer* – Don Johnston (Mac, PC), *TextHelp* – Lorien (PC)
Prediction utilities that work alongside any word processor and offer a list of words as letters are typed. This can reduce the effort for the physically disabled and offer support for those with reading and spelling difficulties. All the above programs have speech facilities, learn new words and adapt the list of words offered to suit the vocabulary of the user. This helps in encouraging the use of subject-specific words for those who have literacy problems.

Writing with Symbols – Widgit (Acorn, PC) Mike Detheridge
Talking animated alphabet.

A word processor that matches symbols to words as they are typed. Can aid understanding and work recorded and, when used for teaching materials, enable poor readers to follow instructions, etc. The word processor has speech output and can be used to enable users to have spoken instructions in combination with text and symbols.

Teaching and Learning Styles

Structuring effective D&T projects

Typically, a D&T Scheme of Work is made up of a range of different projects or units of work to cover the Programme of Study. The D&T projects that teachers use vary from school to school, according to interests and staff expertise. Each project should have a clear focus on teaching particular objectives. As a key stage set, they should cover the National Curriculum requirements in sufficient breadth and in a balanced and progressive way. An appropriate topic should be selected for the project or unit of work to teach knowledge and skills. These projects can be taken from their own ideas, and the DfES/ QCA Schemes of Work Units. Some of these are more appropriate for pupils with special needs than others because they are easier to adapt and differentiate the tasks and the outcome. (Example long-term planning sheets are provided in Appendix 5.1 on the CD which accompanies this book.)

The examples of design and make assignments (DMAs) in this chapter have been taught by a number of schools and they have suggestions about how to adapt them for pupils with SEN. The range of projects were chosen against a number of considerations:

- They are popular amongst pupils with SEN: we asked pupils which projects they had found motivating and interesting.

- They are manageable for the teachers and pupils because the outcome can be controlled so that the quality of the end product is good, but also so there are real opportunities for the pupil to make design decisions and work independently.

- They offer opportunity for full coverage of the D&T National Curriculum Order across the set.

- They provide a range of materials (food, textiles, resistant materials), contexts, experiences and products.

- They offer progression in D&T capability.

- They are flexible to suit different schools.

- They require equipment and expertise from teachers which are normally available (teachers in special schools often work in one room, using a range of materials).

A checklist to use when considering projects at Key Stage 3

(Taken from the National Strategy Foundation Subjects D&T National Programme)

Across the range of projects for the key stage it is important that, amongst them, pupils consider:

Tomorrows' technology	Are long
Intervening to improve the quality of life	Are focused (focused practical tasks)
Working as a team member	Are open (design and make assignments)
Aesthetics	Involve designing but not making
Technical issues	Involve making but not designing
Social issues	Involve product analysis
Environmental issues	Start at various points in the design process
Industrial practices	Are set in a variety of contexts
Present D&T – its uses and effects	Take account of gender issues in relation to D&T tasks
Past D&T – its uses and effects	
Include units which:	**Involve pupils in designing and making:**
Aid transition from Y6 to Y7	'desirable' products
Aid transition from Y9 to Y10	'culturally, environmentally and socially defensible' products
Are short	

Figure 5.1 *A checklist for Key Stage 3 projects*

Selecting appropriate parts of the Programme of Study

The guidance *Planning, teaching and assessing the curriculum for pupils with learning difficulties, D&T* (QCA 2001) www.nc.uk.net/ld specifies appropriate activities and opportunities at each key stage. For example, at Key Stage 3, the PoS focus is working towards these aspects, to give pupils opportunities to:

- suggest outline plans for designing and making

- communicate design proposals

- select and use tools, equipment and processes, including CAD/CAM

- explore the properties of a range of contrasting materials

- analyse products and judge the quality of others people's products

Key Stage 3 expectations

While that is the teaching focus, not all pupils will achieve those things. However, given these opportunities, pupils should be able to:

- make choices about a product or aspects of its design

- observe, explore and experience a range of materials and tools

There are some parts of the PoS that may be too demanding, for example, at Key Stage 3:

- generating design proposals

- prioritising actions and reconciling decisions as a project develops

- considering the chemical and physical qualities of materials

- understanding systems and control or structures

This is not to say that pupils will not study these aspects, for example, *structures,* but that the Key Stage 3 PoS expectation of 'calculate the effects of loads, forces of compression, tension, torsion, shear' was not appropriate. This is not intended to ignore important aspects, but a simple recognition that it is better to focus on the most appropriate to meet the needs of the pupil.

Units of work – examples of projects adapted for pupils with SEN

These principles, then, link to the DfES/QCA Scheme of Work unit examples which follow. They are intended to provide clear case studies of how to adapt the units of work. It was felt essential that the units of work that these pupils engage on are the same as their peers.

Snacks project

Adapting the DfES/QCA Scheme of work Unit 7B(i) Designing and Making for Yourself

Design and make assignment

Design a new and appetising filling for a pasty, which a target group of customers will want to buy. Develop your ideas by tasting other pasties and finding out what customers want. Experiment with different ingredients for the fillings, and test them to help you design something new and tasty for the customers.

Learning objectives

Pupils will be taught to:

- use a range of cutting, shaping and mixing processes

- use a variety of techniques to prepare and process food

- work hygienically in the classroom

- use simple prototypes and modelling to evaluate design ideas

The context

The teacher chose this project because pasties are a familiar product for the pupils and they have eaten them before. The task helps them to develop important manipulative skills. It focuses on designing just the filling and this makes it manageable. It can be extended to include the shape of the finished pasty. The project provides an opportunity for all pupils to achieve a good result. Ready made (fresh or frozen pastry) can be used.

    As this project focuses on the filling preparation, it is possible to substitute a baked potato for the pasty.

Expectations

- Identify possible filling ingredients and mixes of ingredients.

- Evaluate the taste of a range of pasties which can be bought in shops.

- Improve preparation skills, such as cutting and rolling out.

- Select and use appropriate simple food-processing techniques safely.

- Consider safety and hygiene when handling food.

Some pupils may also:

- understand and apply their understanding of what happens when food cooks
- develop ideas and be creative
- work out the costs

Hints and tips

Differentiating the focused practical tasks and managing the design and make assignment

There is a case study of this project and copy of the support sheets that the teacher used in Appendix 5.2 on the CD that accompanies this book.)

- This can be a short project over one or two lessons or a longer project if pupils try out a number of ideas.

- Have a tasting and investigation session – 'What exists already?' on the variety of pasties available. Identify the ingredients in the filling and how they might have been prepared (cut, grated, sliced, mashed). Talk about who would eat which pasty (introducing target market) and when it might be eaten (time of day/purpose). Record responses for the class. Some pupils can record their own responses (a pro-forma sheet might help), others can be assisted in recording – digital photos and key word prompts may help.

- Before pupils begin designing their own ideas use a standard (prototype) recipe to make simple pasties as a class activity, led by the teacher step by step. These will help pupils to understand the limitations of what a pasty is like, what you can put in and what you cannot. They will gain confidence and be more creative in their ideas. They will also be well equipped to plan their own making.

- Have a photo/picture recipe to follow and reinforce key words for equipment, ingredients and processes.

- To reinforce planning, cut the recipe into strips and ask pupils to put them in the right order.

- Minimise the number of stages required in a recipe by pre-preparing some parts of it – using some ready-cut ingredients, using ready-cut circles of pastry. It is important not to do too much for the pupils – this will depend on their ability.

- Templates can be used to make pastry circles – such as a small plate. Uneven rolling out can be prevented by using blocks which have been made for this purpose to the required thickness and balancing the rolling pin on them.

- Understanding how much filling will go into each pasty can be a difficult concept and will require guidance.

- Spend some time exploring and explaining changes in food when it is cooked, using the correct terms where possible (melts, softens, hardens, browns, shrinks, etc.). Challenge pupils to apply their understanding to their own designing by asking them questions: 'Why are you cutting the onion so small?' 'What happened to the cheese?' 'Should you grate the cheese or cut into cubes?' 'Why do you use minced beef?' 'Which will look better?'

- Inspire pupils with a collection of real or photographed ingredients which they could use for the filling. Challenge them to name them by providing the labels to put on.

- Encourage them to develop their design and modify it as they make it. They can record the recipe afterwards.

- Have pro-forma sheets or a spreadsheet to work out the cost of the recipe. With some pupils you can compare the cost of the recipe and the cost in the shops and talk about manufacturing costs and profit.

Disk case/Wallet project

Adapting the DfES/QCA Scheme of Work Unit 8B(iii) Designing for Clients

Design and make assignment

Design and make a wallet or small case for a particular purpose, e.g. to carry computer disks, to hold coins or credit cards, to hold keys or to hold pencils. Develop a standard prototype and then show how it can be adapted simply to make a number of new products for different users, e.g. by using decoration, different fabrics or fastenings, and how it can be batch produced.

Learning objectives

Pupils will be taught:

- batch production, and how basic design can be personalised for a particular person or client

- how to use a template/pattern

The context

The teacher chose this project because each pupil achieves a high quality product that they can make for their own use. In addition to the pleasure of making something to keep and use, the project helps pupils understand the properties of textiles, and the ways in which fabrics can be constructed to fulfil a purpose (such as protection). There is an opportunity to teach valuable construction – using patterns, pinning, cutting out fabric, sewing by hand and machine skills. It is further enhanced when the pupils are able to use CAD/CAM embroidery machines to personalise the disk case/wallet as this will give it a professional finish.

The task can be extended to include work on knitted and woven fabrics, and fabric tests such as absorbency and stretch, as the results are visible and concrete.

To make the making aspects manageable, the pupils are limited to one style of disk case/wallet. A pattern template is provided for this and all the pupils will be making the same style of disk case/wallet after the class agrees on the design. With the case style fixed, pupils will focus on other design decisions such as colour, decorations and fastening.

Expectations

- Evaluate existing disk cases and holders in a product evaluation.

- Choose the colour, fabrics and fastenings.

- Design their own personalisation to decorate the disk case.

- Model the design in paper or inexpensive fabric before making so that the pupil is then able to plan the order of making and test out their idea.

- Use a sewing machine assisted by a helper where needed.

- Use a simple pattern.

Hints and tips

Differentiating the focused practical tasks and managing the design and make assignment

- Provide a range of disk cases for the pupils to evaluate. For example, ask pupils to bring fabric purses, disk holders, pencil cases. If you are limiting the group to making one product, take care that pupils do not think that they can make other types of cases. Talk about – 'What materials are used?' 'How is it fastened?' 'How is it finished?' 'How does it protect the contents?' 'How does it organise the contents?' 'How many parts are there?' 'How is it assembled/in what order?' 'How big is it; is it easy to use?' 'How would you recognise that it is yours?' Record responses for the class, a digital camera and pro-forma sheet can be used. Record key words and information that will help pupils generate design ideas.

- Spend some lessons making simple items to practise using a sewing machine to produce straight seams and hems. Some pupils will be able to learn how to set up a sewing machine. Pictorial instructions will help them. Reward pupils who can do this with a class mentor badge or certificate.

- Pupils may need demonstrations, advice and possibly practice at making seams and hems, depending on their previous experience. Pupils need to be fairly skilful with the machine and may need practice at straight lines. Some pupils will need adult assistance to sew, but the adult should act under the instructions of the pupil.

- Have the pattern templates ready for the pupils to cut out.

- It is important the pupils work out the sequence for making the case. Putting the decoration and pockets on the main part of the bag before sewing it together are key concepts. A jumbled-up flow diagram of the stages with pictures and key words would be very helpful.

- Transferring the seamline (sewing line) from the pattern to the fabric with chalk, transfer wheel or tacking, would be vital for pupils with co-ordination difficulties.

- It may be helpful, depending on the ability of the pupil, to limit the choice of fabric to ones that fray as little as possible (for example, fleece and PVC are very good).

- Provide a limited selection of fasteners for pupils to choose from.

- Pupils will need help with designing the logos, simple scan and sew machines are helpful, and simple stencils and inkjet transfers can be used if no computerised sewing machine is available.

- CAD/CAM embroidered designs can be embroidered onto a piece of fabric which is sewn onto the disk case/wallet. This allows pupils to improve their design, and mistakes on the embroidery will not affect the whole product.

Colouring textiles project

Adapting the DfES/QCA Scheme of work Unit 8A(iii) Exploring Materials (finding an identity) and 8C Using ICT to Support Making (T-shirt challenge)

Design and make assignment

Colour is one of the most exciting parts of designing. We notice colours of food, of clothes, of cars, of shampoo, of everything. We all have our favourite colours and they can make us feel calm, happy, gloomy . . .

Develop your own colourful design on fabric and use it to make a bag, T-shirt or wall hanging. Investigate some of the ways of colouring fabric – tie and dye, batik, block printing.

Learning objectives

Pupils will be taught to:

- identify suitable materials and techniques, taking into account appearance and function

- name and describe the methods and processes used to colour fabrics

- use decorative techniques for a purpose

The context

The teacher chose this project because pupils can respond flexibly: it is adaptable to school situation and pupil ability. It develops important decorative and creative skills.

Pupils may achieve better results with this design and make assignment if the outcome is limited to a particular product (such as T-shirt, shorts, bag). The emphasis is then on learning about different colouring techniques, and applying this knowledge to enhancing their own designed product.

Expectations

- Explore colours and their meanings.

- Explore a range of colouring techniques.

- Choose one technique or a combination to use on their product.

- Choose colours and colour combinations for their product.

Hints and tips

Differentiating the focused practical tasks and managing the design and make assignment

- This is a great opportunity to explore colour in fabrics! Spend some time exploring colour on different textiles products with the pupils. Talk about the different colours, how the colour has been put onto the fabric, the patterns. It is an opportunity to link with art, and look at colour wheels and colour mixing. Colour boards for each colour could be developed, to produce a classroom display. If there is time, pupils could also work with natural dyes from berries and leaves they have collected.

- Developing awareness of colours can be achieved by:
  - weaving with coloured paper to find good colourways
  - wrapping different colours of yarn around card to see what effects can be achieved with a limited range
  - using the computer to produce quick effective moods/atmospheres on the same image

- using wrapping paper/wallpaper fabrics to see why colours are good together

- Use examples to get pupils thinking about 'meaning' in colour.

- Spend some time exploring the techniques first. Pupils may start this project by exploring and experimenting with the different colouring techniques. The making of samples is a motivating end product in itself. It is helpful to record the steps using a digital camera to remind the pupils later. It may be found that if they know the 'product' too soon, they don't explore as readily. Once they have practised batik, tie & dye, and block printing, they could design using the techniques for the range of outcomes – be it T-shirt, sarong, bag, etc. – and then select which they prefer and which they're most successful at.

- The focus is on simple techniques which the pupils must organise well.

- Have some examples of decorated products on display, clearly labelled with the technique used – for discussion and evaluation, and to get ideas.

- Choose fabric carefully as synthetic fibres resist natural dyes.

- Tjantings are quite difficult to use. Make wax paintbrushes by attaching foam to pea sticks with wire.

- When tie dyeing, use elastic bands instead of string to make tying easier.

- Steep ends of garments into a tub of dye – allow pupils to watch colour creep up.

- The T-shirt/bag can be ready made if time is limited or the making skills are learned as part of another DMA.

- Plan the decorating of the final product by talking about it as a group.

'Keeping it under control' project

Adapting the DfES/QCA Scheme of work Unit 7D Using Control to Control a Display

Design and make assignment

A stage play, a pop concert, an animated story or a puppet theatre all involve performances. Presentations to attract people to an event or advertise a product can use animation and other performance techniques. Many museums and theme parks have interactive displays. The best way of producing these effects is to use different types of control systems.

Your challenge is to combine mechanical, electronic, and electrical systems to produce a working model that could be used in a performance or presentation.

Learning objectives

Pupils will be taught:

- how to work as a team to produce a performance

- how to produce a working model

- how systems require control and how this can be achieved

- basic principles of control systems

- how to make structures strong

The context

The teachers chose this project because they were confident in the area of control and wanted a flexible and easily adapted project for different needs that would motivate pupils. It is possible to run it as a group project. It provides important coverage of systems and control and structures aspects of the D&T curriculum.

Systems and control is a complex area with some abstract concepts that make it more difficult for some pupils. Some projects such as 'Keeping it under control' can be very open ended so the teacher sets limits on the outcomes expected from the pupils, while at the same time allowing them some freedom to explore their own ideas.

To make the project meaningful it can be put into a relevant context, for example:

- The puppets could be used to provide a performance for other pupils or young children.

- The toys could be for a particular young child or for a playgroup.

- The display could be for use around the school, in a community building or local library or museum. It could be used to provide information for a particular group of people or in a particular location.

Expectations

- Recognise simple electrical and mechanical control in existing products, for example a lever in a pop-up book.

- Construct simple electrical control circuits that include switches and outputs in parallel and series, protection of LEDs and reversing control of motors.

- Explore four different kinds of motion and how mechanisms can be used to change one kind of motion into another.

- Use cams and linkages.

- Model a strong structure.

Hints and tips

Differentiating the focused practical tasks and managing the design and make assignment

(An example of how lessons can be differentiated according to pupil level is given in Appendix 5.3 on the CD which accompanies this book.)

- Use a series of pictures or examples of models/products that pupils can make. This should lead to each pupil coming up with a realistic and manageable task for themselves.

- Pupils will probably believe that anything to do with control is too difficult. They need to be shown simple examples of control systems and products. Use demonstrations and a display of a range of 'control products', mechanical and electrical toys, puppets, labour saving gadgets, etc. Visit a museum and/or interactive science centre.

- Pupils may need help with planning as they may find it hard to see the need to work in a sequence of stages which need to be planned in advance. Break the project down into smaller steps. Use a planner with key words and pictures of the main stages to help pupils order the sequence of actions. In system and control, the key planning should include working through the following sequence and discussing the possibilities with pupils:
  – What do I want to happen? (Output)
  – How can I make this happen? (Device to use)
  – What do I want to cause it to happen? (Input)

- Use electronic systems kits, mechanical kits, Polymek and other pre-manufactured structural components to help pupils achieve an outcome quickly.

- When making, some pupils will find it hard to work to the level of accuracy required, e.g. making mechanical linkages, or assembling electronic circuits. Make use of as many standard components as possible. Have the Printed Circuit Boards (PCBs) made elsewhere: this would be an excellent task for a group of GCSE/GNVQ pupils. Use a well-labelled container for electronic components (use pictures), and paper soldering equipment including clamps, etc.

- Fault finding in electronics requires patience and a systematic approach. Encourage pupils and show them how to modify things that do not work well first time. Explain that this is part of the process rather than being a failing on their part! Fault finding is a systematic process in which you start at the input and work through each sub-system. Use a simple easy-to-read multimetre with a digital display. You will need to do this with individual circuits. Try to avoid a problem in the finished product by quality control during assembly.

Sheet material project

Adapting the DfES/QCA KS3 Scheme of work Unit 8E(ii) Producing Batches

Design and make assignment

Many products are made from a single sheet of material, e.g. flat sheets can be folded to form a 3D shape to make furniture, containers or packaging. Objects made from folded sheets can be very light and rigid, and folding flat sheets to form a 3D object can be more economical in production than joining separate sections. Complicated shapes can be modelled in card or on computer screens.

Design and make a product that is mainly made from a single sheet of material. Your product should be aimed at the young teenage market and be easily batch produced.

Learning objectives

Pupils should learn:

- that products are designed to meet particular consumer needs

- how to use a range of cutting and shaping processes, selecting and using hand tools to cut, join and shape specific materials safely and accurately

- that manufacturing aids, e.g. jigs and templates, ensure accuracy and help with volume production

- to choose suitable materials and an appropriate method of making

The context

The teacher chose this project because it is easy to relate to pupils' needs and lives. It covers important practical skills and a range of sheet materials. It gives pupils a good foundation in working with a range of materials and processes, and in their understanding of structures, but it can be easily adapted to be challenging and demanding at an appropriate level. It could be a group project.

This project involves pupils designing and making products in sheet plastic (probably acrylic), sheet wood and sheet metal. They explore the properties of materials. One approach is to show the pupils some examples of products they can make. Everyday products are best for introducing this project. Depending on ability, the teacher can limit these to a simple outcome, such as a letter rack, desk tidy or clock. This will make it easier to manage but still give the pupils some choice of product and overall design.

Expectations

- Get ideas by looking at existing products.

- Model ideas in card.

- Explore how sheet material behaves.

- Choose the sheet material and technique for cutting, folding, joining and finishing.

- Assemble their own product.

Hints and tips

Differentiating the focused practical tasks and managing the design and make assignment

- Ask the pupils to work out, and talk with them about, how the products are made, why they are made that way and what materials are used.

- Use a planner sheet with key words and stages to get the pupils started on their design work and also to help them plan their designing and making.

- Encourage straight line bending and circular holes to ease production.

- Make up some jigs and formers in advance.

- When working in acrylic, always drawer file, scrape, wet and dry with 800 paper, and buff to a shine.

- Layers of thin 1mm plywood can be glued together while being held in shape by a former to produce very interesting and strong shapes.

- Health and safety – the edges of sheet metal and other materials may be very sharp: always make sure pupils file a safe edge before they start working the metal and after any cuts are made.

'Puzzling boxes' project

Adapting the DfES/QCA KS3 Scheme of work Unit 7B(ii) Puzzle in a Box

Design and make assignment

Many small gifts, games and puzzles are produced to appeal to a particular group or type of person, e.g. 'Kinder eggs' contain a surprise gift for young children inside a chocolate egg.

The BB Box Company has asked you to make a box of a maximum size $100 \times 100 \times 100$mm. They would also like you to design an interesting gift and finish it in a suitable way.

Learning Objectives

Pupils learn how to:

- use simple prototypes, mock ups and models to evaluate design ideas

- use a range of cutting, forming and shaping processes, e.g. sawing, line bending

- use specified hand tools to cut and form material safely

- use CAD/CAM to make a puzzle aimed at a particular user

The context

The teacher adapted this project easily so that it was very appropriate for pupils with special needs. A simple box is made to a given size. The whole group of pupils can make the same box, and this aspect of the project can be teacher led, step by step. While the box is limited, designing puzzle and decoration provides opportunity for differentiation. Pupils have the opportunity to design and make a high-quality finished outcome that they will be proud of, by using CAD/CAM machines to design and make their puzzle. However, it is possible to do this project without a CAD/CAM machine if schools do not have these facilities.

Expectations

The pupil's design input is focused on being able to:

- cut the lid to suit the chosen purpose of the box

- finish the outside of the box appropriately for the person/purpose they are designing for

- develop a puzzle to fit inside the box also appropriate for the person/purpose

Hints and tips

Differentiating the focused practical tasks and managing the design and make assignment

- The size and the shape of the box that the pupils will make will be a major constraint on the type of puzzle that the pupils design and make to go in it. A successful approach is to make the box first with no reference to the puzzle, simply telling the pupils that the box will be needed for the next part of the project. Being able to see the box has been shown to help many pupils in the design of the puzzle.

- The puzzle box is made as a rectangular or square tube with ends on, which is then cut into two 'halves'. The dimensions of the box can be carefully chosen so that it can be cut in two with a band saw or Hegner saw (power saw to be supervised by the teacher at all times). Birch plywood is the preferred material because of the range of finishes that can be obtained. MDF is also suitable and has some advantages in cutting and sanding. The use of 6mm ply for the two sides and 4mm for the other pair has proved valuable. If the glue is applied to the 6mm ends greater surface adhesion is obtained. It has been found satisfactory to use 1.5mm ply for the end pieces since it is very easy to trim and sand to a good finish.

- When the box has been made, but before the lid is cut off, stand on the boxes to test them. Obviously the box must be upright but this really impresses the pupils, makes them realise the strength of plywood and modern adhesives, demonstrates quality control and, above all, is a bit of fun because they all pass the test if the correct construction procedure has been followed.

- By using different cuts and ink stains, a highly constrained box becomes a unique product. Have a few examples to show the pupils.

- Make a few first, yourself, then try different things such as the type of finish, the number of inserts, different puzzles, etc. This will give you an understanding of the difficulties that may occur and provide a range of examples that may be used to motivate the pupils.

- When the lid has been cut off, hardboard can be used to make the inserts. One on each side is best, but two on opposite sides will do.

- Introduce the puzzle part of the project by asking the pupils to evaluate a variety of puzzles aimed at children and adults. Ask them who they have been designed for. What is the purpose of the puzzle?

- Use lightweight card to model the puzzles and try them out in the box.

- If you do not have a CAD/CAM machine, still design the puzzles on a computer, then print the design, cut it out to make a template, and stick it to the material being used to make the puzzle.

- Don't be put off by the CAD/CAM aspect of this project. If you have CAD/CAM machines it is an ideal way to get you and the pupils started, if not then the alternative method mentioned above really works well and still gives pupils a good, worthwhile experience.

Classy casting – art deco jewellery project

Adapting the DfES/QCA KS3 Scheme of work Unit 8C Using ICT to Support Making (Computer Pewter)

Design and make assignment

Art deco is the name given to a style which was in fashion during the 1920s and 30s. Designs from this period are usually based on combinations of very simple geometric shapes.

Using pictures of art deco designs, create an attractive piece of jewellery which is up to date enough to be worn on a special occasion.

Learning objectives

Pupils will learn:

- how designers rework old and existing ideas to come up with something new

- about an important period of twentieth-century design history

- how metal casting can be used, specifically how cuttlefish moulds are used to cast pewter

The context

The teacher chose this project because it encourages pupils to use source material to develop simple ideas. While drawing skills are included, they are not necessary as pupils can design into the mould. They produce high quality outcomes which are quite easy to achieve. It introduces, in an effective way, principles of casting in metal and industrial manufacturing. Pupils are proud of their jewellery!

The context of art deco requires pupils to look at existing designs to help them design something new. The ability and motivation levels will determine the depth of study and the time spent on looking at design style and generating their own designs.

Expectations

- Use art deco pictures to create an idea for a shaped piece of jewellery.

- Carve their shape into cuttlefish bone mould.

- Make their shape by casting with pewter and attach the findings.

- Clean, buff and polish their jewellery.

Hints and tips

Differentiating the focused practical tasks and managing the design and make assignment

- Have a range of source material of the art deco period to show to the pupils.

- Show the pupils how to go from a picture in source material to a sketch of an idea, for example by simplifying a shape (outlining), or by masking (part of a shape, or magnifying). Photocopied images are useful for simplifying.

- Bold shapes will lessen problems with filing and polishing. Intricate shapes are likely to bend and snap.

- It is possible to go straight to the modelling stage using card or playdough, etc. to help pupils develop their ideas if they are not good at sketching. The modelling helps the pupils understand how they will need to sculpt their mould. The bits on the model that stand out furthest will have to be cut the deepest.

- A plan of the process step by step will be helpful.

- The teacher will need to prepare the cuttlefish bone. Any good pet shop will let you have a box of cuttlefish bones at trade price. Unfortunately, it can make the storeroom a bit smelly. When cutting the top off the cuttlefish bone, use a hacksaw and cut from the hard side. This prevents the cuttlefish bone cracking and splitting. (Every cuttlefish bone has a hard side and a soft side.)

- Instead of using cuttlefish bone, layers of hardboard can be used.

- Flatten the soft side of the cuttlefish bone for sculpting the mould. This needs to be done on sandpaper. Don't rub back and forwards because you get a curved surface. Put the cuttlefish bone on the sandpaper and pull it towards you and repeat until one side is flat.

- Show the pupils how to sculpt the mould with a used ballpoint pen and shake the dust off as they go. Protective glasses should be worn. Using a ballpoint pen can enable good detail and it is easy to control. Don't touch the flat surface or the sculpted mould shape with your hands because it is so soft that the shape can easily be damaged.

- Pewter has a comparatively low melting point so you do not need a brazing hearth. If you have a dedicated casting/heat treatment area, it is best to use it. Small camping gas stoves and even domestic hobs have been used but health and safety issues must be observed. A large biscuit tin with dry sand in it can be used to stand the cuttlefish bones in for pouring. This provides a safe environment for any spillage and the spill can be reclaimed when cold. All modern pewter is lead free, old pewter is not.

Corporate identity project

Adapted from QCA/DfES Unit 9C Using ICT to Link with the World Outside School

Design and make assignment

Souvenirs and collectables, e.g. T-shirts, 3D signs and models, are used to promote events, pop stars, cartoon characters and even schools.

Design and make a co-ordinated range of promotional products for a special occasion or a client. You should work in a team and produce at least three different products using a range of materials.

Learning objectives

Pupils will learn:

- to use ICT effectively when working on a collaborative project

- to use ICT to research and analyse information and expertise from outside the school and to collect appropriate information for their project, e.g. examples of logos

- to develop teamwork skills

- to use CAD/CAM

The context

The teacher chose this project because a range of outcomes are possible and individual pupils' responses are easy to accommodate. Corporate and promotional products are easy to source and give pupils many ideas. The teacher can focus the project on a real class or school event to give the pupils context that they can relate to. It is also possible to make the researching and designing of the logo or corporate image a whole-class designing activity. The individuals then use the design to make their own products. The same logo/image can be printed, embroidered or milled onto products according to the ability of the pupil. The teacher restricted this activity to produce a banner or T-shirt, but allowed the pupils to make many of their own design decisions.

Expectations

In bringing together what they have learned to make a promotional T-shirt or banner:

- Choose an appropriate image and text to be used.

- Choose the colours.

- Choose the method of transferring the image and text onto the T-shirt or banner.

- Use an on-screen grid to select words and symbols while others use the keyboard.

- With help, use a computer embroidery machine.

- With help, practise screen printing and use of fabric crayons/pens.

Hints and tips

Differentiating the focused practical tasks and managing the design and make assignment

- Have a range of promotional T-shirts and other items with designs on them to investigate.

- Show the pupils how to use, and let them practise using, a digital camera.

- Show the pupils how to use, and let them produce, images using draw or paint computer software.

- Show the pupils how to use, and let them produce, screen-printing templates using a printer.

- Show the pupils how to use, and let them practise using, a word processor to produce writing and symbols.

'Feeding special groups' project

Adapting the DfES/QCA KS3 Scheme of work Unit 9A(i) Selecting Materials – Specialist diets

Design and make assignment

People demand choice, whether they are eating a meal on an aircraft, in a restaurant or in a motorway service station, and meals and dishes have to be made to suit a range of different dietary needs. Many food outlets buy ready-prepared meals that can be kept frozen or chilled before being served to customers.

A company wants to buy a new meal to offer to customers with special dietary needs. Design a prototype of a suitable dish and present it to the company.

Learning objectives

Pupils will be taught:

- what is meant by a special dietary need, such as vegetarianism

- how foods contribute to a healthy diet – balanced plate food groups

- how to select ingredients according to their nutritional characteristics

- how to combine ingredients for different purposes

- how to work safely and hygienically

The context

The teacher chose this project because nutrition is an important area to cover in food technology. It is often of personal interest as pupils with special needs often have special dietary requirements. This project also promotes understanding of hygiene and safety.

A more focused project was used which looked at the dietary need of vegetarianism. The teacher can choose an appropriate dietary need for the class, rather than allowing pupils the choice to research any of them. This eases management issues which might be encountered if pupils all undertook different dietary needs and ensures that successful products can be designed and made by all pupils. The meal could also be developed by the group with individual pupils contributing different parts of the meal.

Expectations

- Explore, taste and comment on different dishes and recipes that are available for special diets.

- Choose ingredients appropriate to the special diet.

- Assemble ingredients to make a recipe for a special diet.

- Be able to say why they have chosen the ingredients.

Hints and tips

Differentiating the focused practical tasks and managing the design and make assignment

- Provide a supportive structure and show the pupils a manageable way through the tasks. Break up the activity into smaller tasks with specific targets.

- Keep this project short if you need to.

- Evaluate existing vegetarian products to give pupils ideas to help them with their designing. A selection of different types of vegetable burgers could be used for the sensory evaluation test. Alternatively, a range of vegetarian meals, e.g. 'meals for one', could be used to help introduce the ideas of portion control and a 'balanced meal/diet'.

- Investigating products designed for vegetarians makes a good homework activity for some pupils. Pupils could look for the vegetarian symbol. Show a variety from different packaging, e.g. Marks & Spencer, Sainsburys, vegetarian society. An extension of this could be a group activity to produce an information sheet or wall chart or class display for the school on vegetarianism.

- Reduce the amount of reading, researching and written recording required. Simplify and adapt research information, provide key words and pictures. Discuss different dietary needs with flashcards of different people/situations, for example show a picture of breakfast: 'What would a vegetarian have for breakfast?' If possible, have real alternatives/ingredients for the pupils to point to or talk about.

- If an outside visit cannot be arranged, ask the school meal service/community dietician to visit the class. This may help the pupils develop a questionnaire and/or a new item on the school lunch menu. Visiting speakers should be briefed carefully.

- A visit to the school kitchen may enable pupils to see 'hands on', storage areas, health and safety procedures and equipment, e.g. portion control and temperature probes (for pupils to understand food safety).

- Include lots of focused making tasks led by the teacher to set recipe, to build up the pupils' skills.

- Encourage the pupils to choose recipes where they will produce good quality outcomes, so that they build their self-esteem and confidence.

- A mini production line could be devised within the classroom to reinforce this process. Setting up a production line for mass production will be more successful as a group activity. A practical task like 'burgers' could prove to be a popular option.

Soups and salads project

Adapting the DfES/QCA KS3 Scheme of work Unit 7A(i) Understanding Materials (and linking to the KS1/2 Scheme of work Eat more Fruits and Vegetables)

Design and make assignment

Health experts recommend that we eat at least five portions of fruits and vegetables each day to keep our bodies healthy and working properly.

Design and make a new salad or soup which looks good and appeals to customers.

Learning objectives

Pupils will be taught:

- how to classify ingredients, for example by food groups

- how to prepare, cut, mix and heat ingredients safely

- where fruits and vegetables come from, and what they are called (and what their parts are called: roots, stalk, etc.)

- how to find out what people like

The context

The teacher chose this project because it is easy to adapt as a number of simple to increasingly complex products are possible. It provides an opportunity to teach basic food concepts and skills. It is a short project, that can be extended if you wish.

Expectations

Pupils bring together what they have learned to design and make a salad or a soup/drink for themselves.

- They choose from fruits/vegetables provided by the teacher.

- They choose how to prepare and cut them.

Hints and tips

Differentiating the focused practical tasks and managing the design and make assignment

- Provide opportunities for pupils to *investigate familiar products* and explore materials:
    - Observe, touch, smell and taste different fruits and fruit juices and respond to them.
    - Record as a class how many pieces of fruit they eat each day.
    - Collect pictures of fruits and vegetables and label them; use them for choosing ingredients when designing; put them into groups (colours, juicy-not juicy, etc.).
    - Observe fruits/vegetables growing.
    - Observe, touch, smell, taste ready-made products made from fruit/vegetables (for example, canned fruit salad, chilled salad) and respond to these products.
    - Observe and explore changes in fruits (for example, the teacher shows them a raw apple and a cooked apple; the teacher leaves a cut apple to go brown).

- Teach essential practical skills through *focused practical tasks* led by the teacher before the pupils think about designing:
    - For example, with help, pupils wash, clean, peel, cut, slice, grate, squeeze and mix different fruits/vegetables and fruit juices, for example making coleslaw, fruit smoothies to a recipe set by the teacher.
    - Harder food to be chopped or sliced while holding it with a fork or other holding device.

- Use serrated-edged knives rather than smooth-edged knives.

- There is a wide variety of different handled and shaped peelers, etc.

- Use some (but not all) ready prepared ingredients for some pupils.

When supporting designing, provide simple choices from a given range when designing according to the ability of the pupil. Allow pupils to design 'as they make' and make changes as they go along. Have opportunities to try again and modify as this is quite a quick product to make.

Moving stories project

Adapting the DfES/QCA KS3 Scheme of work Unit (and linking to the KS1/2 Winding Up and Storybooks)

Design and make assignment

Design and make a storybook or display that has moving parts for a particular purpose. (Individual teachers add contextual information according to the project they are doing, for example making a story prop which includes a winding mechanism, or design characters for our story so that they look good, can be seen across the room and are easy to attach to the 'winders'.)

Learning objectives

Pupils will be taught how:

- products with lever and linkages systems function

- to use particular mechanisms for a purpose

- to use technical vocabulary to describe the properties of materials and mechanisms, e.g. 'lever', 'pivot', 'linkage'

The context

The teacher chooses a simple mechanisms project for her class by drawing on suggested resources from an earlier key stage unit where appropriate for the pupils. The focus of the project is on introducing the pupils to the concept of winding mechanisms, building on their knowledge of wheels and axles. They explore how to make winding mechanisms using construction kits, then after discussion, make their own, using appropriate materials.

Expectations

Pupils bring together what they have learned to design and make a winding mechanism for a story or display.

- They work as a class, choosing the story, and each child makes a specified part of the design, for example, with appropriate help.

- The teacher provides a template, a choice of designs, or allows the pupil to design their own part, according to their individual needs.

Hints and tips

Differentiating the focused practical tasks and managing the design and make assignment

- Provide opportunities for pupils to *investigate familiar products* and explore materials:
  - Observe and explore simple winding mechanisms in a range of toys.
  - Observe how the mechanism works and respond to the movement of the mechanism.
  - Become aware of the different parts, such as wheel, axles, winder, pulley and gears.

- Teach essential practical skills through *focused practical tasks* led by the teacher before the pupils think about designing:
  - With help, build a winding mechanism using construction kit parts.
  - Practise controlling the mechanism and become aware of cause and effect (if they turn the winder, the pulley winds the cord around it and the hook rises).
  - Explore ways to pick up items such as a bucket, magnet or hook.
  - With help, measure and cut small-section timber or dowel.
  - With help, assemble parts, such as joining axles to base, and wheel to axles.

Musical instruments project

Adapting the DfES/QCA KS1/2 Scheme of work Unit 5A Musical Instruments

Design and make assignment

Design and make a musical instrument to accompany a performance.

Learning objectives

Pupils will be taught:

- how musical instruments function

- what materials and methods of assembly are used to make instruments

- how different sounds are made

- how to join and combine materials accurately

The context

The teacher chose a simple mechanisms project for this class by drawing on suggested resources from an earlier key stage unit where appropriate for the pupils. The focus of the project is on learning about musical instruments from different times and cultures, and how different sounds are created and altered to make different notes. The project links with work that the pupils are doing in music and science. A wide range of simple to complex instruments are possible, enabling pupils to respond at their own level and participate fully in the project.

Expectations

Pupils work on a *design and make assignment* as a class and bring together what they have learned to design and make a musical instrument to accompany a piece of music, or for sound effects for a story. They work as a class, choosing the story or sound effects, and each child makes a specified sound or instrument, with appropriate help. According to the pupils' individual needs the teacher:

- provides a template and a plan to make a specified instrument

- allows the pupil to choose elements of the design (such as a choice of three different bottles, three different fillings for a shaker, three different beaters or choice of colours)

- allows the pupil to design their own instrument within a given range of materials and tools

Hints and tips

Differentiating the focused practical tasks and managing the design and make assignment

- Provide opportunities for pupils to *investigate familiar products* and explore materials:
  - Make sounds or respond to sounds made by different musical instruments.
  - Feel the different materials that are used to make the musical instruments.

> – Become aware of different parts of existing musical instruments, such as box, arm, stem, board, string.

- Teach essential practical skills through *focused practical tasks* led by the teacher before the pupils think about designing:
  - Experiment with making sounds, for example shakers (margarine pots with rice, gravel or sand), scrapers (plastic bottles with ridges, dowelling and glasspaper), drums (food containers, biscuit tins, materials stretched over the top of boxes), string instruments (food containers, elastic bands, string).
  - Investigate which part makes the noise, become aware of how to control the noise and make different sounds or notes.

Case studies reflecting examples of good practice

(A checklist for adapting Schemes of work units is in Appendix 5.4 on the CD that accompanies this book.)

- Units of work from the QCA/DfES Scheme of work are selected where it is known that pupils will achieve a good end product in a context that motivates them.

- The projects have clearly focused objectives for the whole class and each pupil.

- The Units of work have been differentiated appropriately to meet the needs of individual pupils. There are different expectations for individuals within a group from the outset, with planned extension work to challenge some pupils and adult and peer support for others where needed.

- There is a full range of activities provided, such as focused practical tasks, product evaluation, and design and make assignments.

- Aspects of the project are directed and structured by the teacher, but planned opportunities for pupils to be responsible for certain aspects of designing and decision making are incorporated. The teacher allows as much independence as possible.

- Longer projects are broken down into smaller achievable stages. There are many mini-making activities for pupils to motivate them and build up their confidence.

- Much designing is done with real materials and done actively: there is less reliance on drawing and presenting ideas on paper.

- Cross-curricular links and learning from other subjects or topics is used effectively to save time and enable pupils to apply learning in other contexts.

- ICT is used to support learning and to provide a means for recording and presenting work more quickly so that time is gained for other activities.

(A template for a project proforma is supplied in Appendix 5.5 on the CD which accompanies this book.)

Case study: Wood Lane School's pasties

(Examples of the support sheets that were used for this project are included in Appendix 5.2 on the CD that accompanies this book.)

Three Key Stage 3 groups of children at Wood Lane School were involved in the 'Snacks – Pasty' DMA , which asks children to 'design a new and appetising filling for a pasty which customers will want to buy'.

The project was adapted for a child with significant visual impairment and then again modified for other Key Stage 3 children. These children had a wide range of barriers: medical, language, co-ordination, development, emotional fragility or a combination of these, bringing with them resultant learning disabilities. Teaching groups had a wide range of ability and quite differing dynamics.

Researching the origins of Cornish pasties led children to quickly make links with geography and history. Map work and stories about tin miners helped to establish the context of the assignment. Visits to local supermarkets helped to reinforce the purpose of the project. The children were able to generate lots of possible solutions to the problem and were clear about the criteria the *design brief* set for success. Saving wrappers, containers and labels that the products came in helped the children to generate their own design ideas when designing packaging for homework assignments.

The commercial nature of the project and carrying out sensory analysis tests on existing pasties further raised the sense of 'quality' that the children felt. It signified the importance of the enterprise and increased the enjoyment the groups were experiencing, working as teams. By taking photographs and getting them displayed quickly, we helped capture the success and pleasure this project was bringing to the children.

The first prototype helped children with modelling ideas, and increased enthusiasm for working in teams supported those children with fine motor control difficulties. They were able to suggest improvements to the prototype recipe which further clarified the task and helped to make it more accessible.

Materials were transferred to *Clicker Plus* which further helped children with significant literacy problems. Some children used this as a back-up by using the speech facility as a way of checking their own understanding.

Scheme of work: 'All Wrapped Up'

Week 1

Introduce the project: 'Design a new and appetising filling for the pasty which customers will want to buy'.

Research: Visit supermarkets and shops to look at the range of pasties (and wrapped foods) already on the market. Investigate pasty fillings. Purchase some for product tasting.

Homework: (a) Design the front of a packet containing three small pasties.

(b) Cornish miners' map or wordsearch.

Week 2

Product evaluation and discussion: Pasty testing/Taste Panel.

Preparation for the questionnaire.

Homework: (a) Write a report or tape a radio programme for a food magazine or show.

(b) Wordsearch

Week 3

Using the questionnaire: 'What do customers want?'

Discuss: Looking at labels.

Sorting out ideas. Concept screening.

Homework: (a) Work on graphs.

(b) What do customers want?

Week 4

Practical: trying out a prototype recipe.

Homework: Complete self-evaluation.

Week 5

Consumer testing 1: What happens when it cooks? (Practical tests).

Evaluation 1: Discuss – how well will the ideas work? Why have particular ingredients been chosen?

Homework: Case Study – Ginsters Ltd.

Week 6

Practical: Prototype 2 (own ideas).

Discuss improvements to a new filling – record a specification.

Homework: Question and answer sheet trying new ideas.

Week 7

Discuss: Consumer testing 2: 'Do your potential customers like the product? How will you find out?'

Evaluation 2: Taste testing and asking others' opinions.

Present your results (can be as a class).

Homework: (a) Complete graph work.

(b) Complete 'finding out'.

(c) Complete evaluation.

Week 8

Simple costing (remember 'Customers will not buy it if it costs too much!')

Discuss: Final evaluation.

Homework: (a) Write a final report.

(b) Complete report evaluation sheet.

(c) Complete packaging for your pasty.

Case study: Working Together Week – Developing partnerships

Queen's Croft Community School is an all-age MLD school catering for 150 pupils. They say that Working Together Week was probably the most exciting week in their history. Thirteen schools took part in a multicultural activity week – five secondary, one secondary PRU, five primary, one independent and a special school. The regular timetable was disbanded and many exciting projects were organised. Experts from a range of backgrounds came into school to lead activities. Staff from each curriculum area planned activities with a multicultural focus for delivery throughout the week.

The aims were to:

- build bridges and open opportunities for racial harmony

- develop tolerance and understanding

- increase knowledge and experience of a variety of cultures

- break down barriers within the community that exist around a special school, through teamwork, parental involvement and with mainstream pupils

- offer stimulating and exciting learning opportunities, by introducing professionals from a variety of cultural backgrounds, with particular areas of expertise

- offer an opportunity for teamwork in inclusive groups, culminating in a celebration of our diversity

This was a whole school activity involving all age groups 5–16 years. A variety of artists were employed for the week:

- an Afro-Caribbean story-teller

- an Afro-Caribbean musician, actor, and story-teller

- an Asian hand painter (Mehndi)

- an Asian artist (Rangoli coloured rice pictures)

- a textile artist

- an Indian dancer (Bhangra)

In addition, staff from each curriculum area planned activities with a multi-cultural focus for delivery throughout the week.

How was it organised?

Each day, 48 pupils arrived – 36 primary and 12 secondary. The schools taking part made sure that the event was high profile – in some cases, pupils had to write a letter of application for a place.

Usual class groups at Queen's Croft were re-organised and 12 new groups were created. Mainstream pupils were added to every group and pupils were

discouraged from wearing uniform so that it was hard to tell where they had come from.

The week ended with a morning at Lichfield Civic Hall, celebrating the diverse activities that had taken place. By exhibiting and sharing work, children were able to demonstrate what they had learnt about other cultures and values during the week.

A colourful array of design-related work was produced during the course of the week. Individual achievements included mobiles, masks, Indian head-dresses, ceramic jewellery, and computer designed T-shirts, place mats and coasters. The pupils made their view of the top of the world (the Arctic Circle) into a 3D model. They used mathematical skills to produce Paisley patterns using rotational symmetry. And they listened to stories from different countries around the world and designed book covers for a competition. The project was deliberately planned to ensure that the skills, experience and expertise of people from local ethnic minority communities were utilised within the curriculum and served as positive role models.

Working as a team

The collaborative projects provided a number of permanent mementos of the week, including:

- a beautiful wall hanging made from textiles, produced using a range of processes

- a frieze depicting a story, made in a day by primary children

- a batik banner made up of 48 sections by different pupils

- clay tiles which, when fired, will be mounted as a mosaic

Each school that was involved in the project will also receive a copy of a newspaper about the week that was compiled by primary reporters.

The pupils had the opportunity to work with people from other cultures. They:

- developed an understanding of different lifestyles

- learned about differing dress style, eating habits and beliefs

- recognised, respected and valued the diversity of humanity

- recognised that every group embraced a range of talents

- developed friendships between mainstream and special pupils

- recognised and celebrated achievement at all levels

Throughout the week, all of the pupils involved in the project learnt, had fun, made new friends and grew in confidence with each other. Evaluations received from pupils have been extremely positive and more than justify the large amount of effort and planning that went into the event. Parents have commented how animated and excited their children were when they came home (not to mention exhausted!). Some said that their child talked more that week than ever before.

When asked, 'What was the most important thing you learnt?', pupils commented:

- 'No matter what school people go to or what may be wrong everyone has a life and feelings to share.'

- 'Working with others and respecting their thoughts and views.'

- 'How to make friends with people from different schools.'

Following up the week – some conclusions

- Staff have had the opportunity to experiment with multicultural activities relating to their subject areas. They can now build them into their schemes of work.

- The week should be repeated, but not as an annual event as first thought, possibly three-yearly.

- Staff have benefited from the experience of the visiting artists.

Case study: Linking with other schools: Bolling Special School and Dixons CTC

When Bolling Special School in Bradford approached Dixons City Technology College, they were looking for opportunities for their 17- and 18-year-old pupils to work alongside similar age pupils in a different environment.

The aims were for pupils to work alongside mainstream pupils at Dixons City Technology College for one morning a week. The groups were introduced to each other before the course started. Pupils took part in learning activities organised by CTC staff and pupils. They accessed the canteen at break times. They travelled to and from the CTC by mini bus.

In successfully completing this unit, the pupils would demonstrate the following abilities:

Setting off

1. Collect own belongings.
2. Find way to mini bus.
3. Sit in own seat.
4. Put seat belt on.
5. Travel in an acceptable manner.
6. Request assistance.

At CTC

7. Recognise and greet pupils.

8. Find way to signing-in desk.

9. Wait turn at desk and remain with group.

10. Find way to cloakroom.

11. Use lift.

12. Use stairs.

13. Find way to learning 'base'.

14. Complete/participate in learning activity.

End of lesson/break

15. Find way to canteen.

16. Use vending machine to buy drink.

17. Behave appropriately in the company of CTC peers.

18. Interact positively with CTC peers.

Dixons CTC is well equipped with extensive workshops and CAD/CAM facilities. It was felt that these offered the opportunity to allow Bolling pupils a different experience and the chance to make good quality products.

Work began with a simple clock which was based on a vacuum-formed plastic body. Each pupil produced the clock body using a range of machinery and assisted by a small group of Dixons pupils. There was no intention of providing any designing activity at this stage. The former had been produced so that the plastic body would offer a good surface area to personalise the product.

The next stage was to use the Corel Draw! computer program to design suitable graphics which would eventually be cut from self-adhesive vinyl on a Roland plotter cutter. A template had been prepared to allow the Bolling pupils to size and space the graphics accurately.

The pupils quickly got to grips with this and, apart from the final positioning onto the clock body and assistance with fitting the mechanism, they raced ahead of schedule. It was at this point that the work took an unexpected turn as there was unplanned time to spare. It was decided that a sign be made for a room at Bolling School, and this developed into a complete signage system which extended the project into another academic year. The Royal Blue plotter-cut vinyl signs were stuck onto yellow polystyrene sheet backing plates which the Bolling pupils cut on a bandsaw and cleaned up carefully. Double-sided tape was applied to each sign so that it could be stuck to a door back at school. Several groups of Bolling pupils took part in the work and it was easy to slot a different group into the signage production, as batches of signs were produced: 'Privacy and Dignity', room numbers, etc.

A year into the partnership and, flushed with success, it was felt that more ambitious work could be undertaken. The Bolling pupils investigated some needs and opportunities back at school and returned with requests for number matching. A Denford milling machine was put to use controlled by MillCAM Designer software and, although this did stretch the Bolling pupils considerably, the results were very professional. A wide range of traditional woodworking machinery such as bandsaws and sanders were employed to complete the task.

While it is clear that Bolling Special School benefited considerably from the partnership, it is perhaps not so obvious what Dixons CTC gained. Several Post-16 pupils worked closely with the Bolling pupils and gained in confidence and maturity as a result. Indeed, two of them went on to undertake GCE A-Level design and technology major projects aimed at children with special needs. Staff have benefited from working with different pupils with different needs and the whole college has benefited from having Bolling pupils take part in normal social events.

The messages are clear. Large secondary schools often have equipment which could benefit special needs schools' pupils. CAD/CAM offers particular benefits in terms of accessibility and quality of results. Mainstream pupils benefit from this type of social interaction and soon become very adept at knowing when to support and when to step back. The only drawback appears to be timetabling. However, Bolling School operates a very flexible programme with its post-16 pupils so, as long as they fitted in with the slack time at Dixons, even that was overcome. It is anticipated that this partnership will continue indefinitely.

CHAPTER 6

Monitoring and Assessment

Planning and reviewing progress

Pupils need to be assured that their successes will be recognised and rewarded and that, when they have difficulty accessing learning, the necessary support will be available. Teachers need to know when things are going well and when they are not, so that they can change their teaching approaches as appropriate. (*SEN: Training materials for the Foundation Subjects*, Introduction, DfES 2003)

Identifying starting points

D&T teachers use a variety of assessment techniques to identify the needs of individual pupils, for example, a standard practical task, observation checklists for development of practical skills, or an opportunity for a pupil to explain or communicate a design idea to the group. It would be rare for the teacher to use a full design and make assignment as an assessment task for pupils with special educational needs, such as the non-statutory tasks and tests (for example 1996 SCAA optional tasks and tests). More appropriate would be a shorter activity that is observed by the teacher, for example following a sequence of instructions to assemble a simple product, or using a chart template and word bank to evaluate and test a set of existing products. These are important to identify starting points from which progress can be measured.

These opportunities help the teacher to gather information about existing knowledge, skills and understanding, as well as strengths and needs, personal interests and how the pupil prefers to learn. The priorities can then be recorded as targets on the IEP in order to determine future priorities and targets. This will also provide valuable indicators regarding how much support the pupils needs to access and complete tasks, which will help with planning resources and support.

For pupils with a statement of special educational need, assessment is part of a continuous cycle, driving the annual review process and providing information to support the development and ongoing review of IEP targets.

Working from the IEP

The IEP is a planning, teaching and reviewing tool. It underpins the process of planning intervention for a pupil with special educational needs.

IEPs should be teaching and learning plans setting out 'what', 'how' and 'how often' particular knowledge, understanding and skills should be taught through additional and different activities from those provided for all pupils through the differentiated curriculum.

The IEP is the structured planning document setting out the steps and teaching required to help pupils achieve identified targets. It should set out short-term targets and strategies, with specified success criteria and outcomes. It is a working document. Setting too many targets at one time is not appropriate: it is best to set up to three or four key targets to help individual needs and priorities. It is often helpful to use phrases such as . . . 'By the end of term, Barrie will be able to . . .'

IEPs should:

- raise attainment

- detail provision additional to or different from that generally available to all pupils

- promote effective planning

- help pupils monitor their own progress

- result in achievement of specific goals for pupils

(taken from SEN Toolkit Section 5 *Managing Individual Education Plans*, DfES 2001)

Writing D&T targets for IEPs

(A useful prompt sheet 'Are your IEP targets SMART?' is provided in Appendix 6.1 on the CD which accompanies this book.)

The booklet *Planning, Teaching and Assessing pupils with Learning Difficulties* (QCA 2001, www.nc.uk.net/ld) provides some useful guidance about what should be included in setting out the 'what' and the 'how' in IEPs at Key Stage 3 and Key Stage 4. Teachers will need to use their knowledge of the pupil to match this to 'how often' and priorities.

OPPORTUNITIES AND ACTIVITIES AT KEY STAGE 3

Much of the D&T Programme of Study at Key Stage 3 is relevant to pupils with learning difficulties. With modification, it can provide stimulating and challenging learning opportunities.

The focus of teaching D&T at Key Stage 3 may be on giving pupils opportunities to:

- suggest outline plans for designing and making
- communicate design proposals
- select and use tools, equipment and processes, including CAD/CAM to shape and form
- use materials safely and accurately and finish them appropriately
- explore the properties of a range of contrasting materials, including resistant materials
- use compliant materials and/or food
- analyse products and judge the quality of other people's products

GIVEN THESE OPPORTUNITIES AT KEY STAGE 3:

all pupils with learning difficulties (including those with the most profound disabilities):

- make choices about a product or aspects of its design
- observe, explore and experience a range of materials and tools

most pupils with learning difficulties (including those with severe difficulties in learning) who will develop further skills, knowledge and understanding in most aspects of the subject:

- suggest next steps when planning
- select and use a variety of tools, equipment and processes
- communicate design proposals in a variety of ways

a few pupils with learning difficulties who will develop further aspects of knowledge, skills and understanding in the subject:

- develop their ideas by taking into account how their products will be used and who will use them
- judge the quality of other people's products

Some parts of the Key Stage 3 Programme of Study may be too demanding for some pupils. These parts may be:

- generating design proposals
- prioritising actions and reconciling decisions as a project develops
- considering the physical and chemical qualities of materials
- understanding systems and control or structures

OPPORTUNITIES AND ACTIVITIES AT KEY STAGE 4

Much of the D&T Programme of Study at Key Stage 4 is relevant to pupils with learning difficulties. With modification, it can provide stimulating and challenging learning opportunities.

The focus of teaching D&T at Key Stage 4 may be on giving pupils opportunities to:

- use graphic techniques and ICT, including CAD, to generate, develop, model and communicate design proposals
- select and use tools, equipment and processes effectively and to make products safely that match a specification
- understand how materials can be combined and processed to create more useful properties
- understand a variety of finishing processes
- ensure that their products are of a suitable quality for intended users and suggest modifications

GIVEN THESE OPPORTUNITIES AT KEY STAGE 4:

all pupils with learning difficulties (including those with the most profound disabilities):

- contribute to design and make projects that are linked to their own interests
- observe, explore and use a range of materials and tools
- combine and process materials

most pupils with learning difficulties (including those with severe difficulties in learning) who will develop further skills, knowledge and understanding in most aspects of the subject:

- communicate their ideas in different ways
- design and make products suitable for the user

a few pupils with learning difficulties who will develop further aspects of knowledge, skills and understanding in the subject:

- take part in projects that are linked to their own interests, industrial practice and the community

Some parts of the Key Stage 4 Programme of Study may be too demanding for some pupils. Such parts may be:

- using design briefs, detailed specifications and criteria
- using a range of industrial applications
- checking design proposals against design criteria
- understanding how to achieve the optimum use of materials and components
- demonstrating a knowledge of systems and control

(Example IEPs are included in Appendix 3.1 on the CD that accompanies this book.)

Monitoring pupils' success against medium-term and short-term objectives

It is helpful to consider both medium-term and short-term objectives for the individual.

- *Medium-term learning objectives* will be set out in an IEP which provide priorities for learning. These may be written as key skill objectives, for example communication and independent learning, or in terms of the pupil's priority needs. A good planning tool or IEP will include success criteria related to these. The objectives and success criteria from the IEP will be reflected in the planning for the unit of work or design and make assignment.

- *Short-term learning objectives* should be clear for individual lessons or tasks such as focused practical tasks or product evaluation activities. For some pupils, objectives should be set for separate episodes of learning within the lesson. These objectives need recognisable success criteria.

Example – Planning and reviewing progress against medium-term learning objectives and success criteria

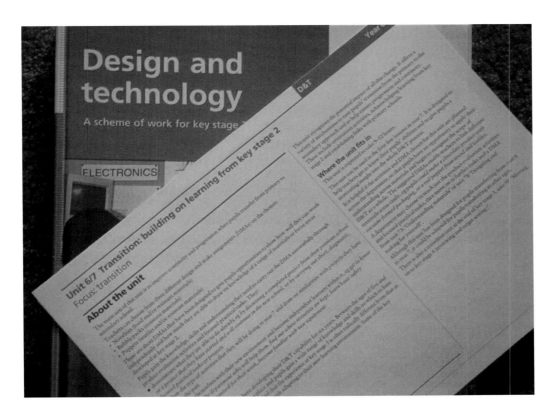

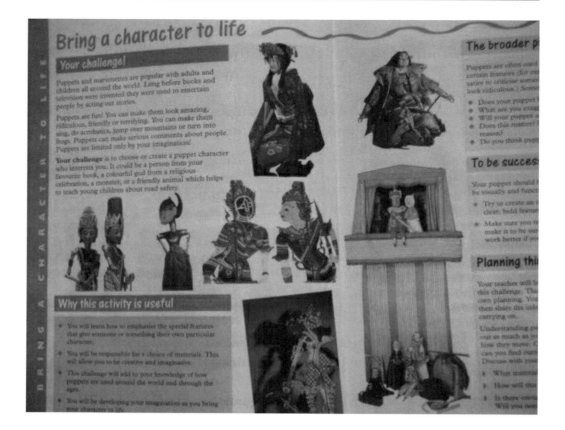

Puppets project

A class teacher is working with some Year 7 pupils on an adapted version of a Puppets design and make assignment taken from QCA/DfES KS3 D&T Scheme of work Unit 6/7 Puppets, and KS1/2 Unit 2B Puppets:

Design and make assignment

Puppets are a good way to help children learn about issues such as crime, avoiding strangers, road safety, keeping teeth clean, healthy eating, and not playing with fire. Produce a puppet and write a story to teach primary school children something useful.

EXPECTATIONS	
at the end of this unit	
most children will:	have discussed their ideas as they developed and be able to say what their design has to do; have created a puppet that works (ie is the right size and reflects the character) using a given technique; have stitched two pieces of fabric together and added features using appropriate materials and techniques
some children will not have made so much progress and will:	have made suggestions as to what they intend to do; have created a puppet with support by gluing two pieces of fabric together and added features using appropriate materials and techniques
some children will have progressed further and will:	have reflected on their own ideas and have worked independently to create their puppet using appropriate techniques to measure, mark out and join the fabric pieces they have selected; have added features to their puppet to capture particular characteristics and expressions; have been able to identify how well the puppet works in relation to simple design criteria

Figure 6.1 *QCA Scheme of work Unit 2B Puppets – Expectations*

The teacher writes an assessment guide sheet (see below):

DMA	**Puppets**

Area(s) of study	**Multi-materials**

To be successful (from student book)

Your puppet should be successful in two ways. It needs to be visually and functionally successful:
- Try to create an interesting and unusual character – with clear, bold features and which comes to life when you use it.

- Make sure you test your puppet out as you design and make it to be sure it will work. Make the changes necessary to make it work better.

Assessment focuses

Designing:
- with the use of colour and texture in a wide range of possible materials
- with simple mechanisms to produce an animated puppet.

Making:
- to quite low levels of difficulty but to high levels of finish.

Teaching focuses

To develop imagination and creativity in students.
To utilise different sources to stimulate these.
To utilise a very wide range of possible materials to develop character.

Designing statements — Advanced

The design folio:
- makes the fullest use of quality drawing and models*
- demonstrates competence in visualisation techniques
- contains a number of designs which are derived from a range of sources.

Ideas portray a character, with vitality*.
Evaluation shows understanding of 'character'.

Intermediate

The design folio includes:
- drawings and/or models to an adequate standard
- competent use of either colours or materials in creating a character.
- a limited number of alternative designs
- some range of design sources.
- A final design proposal is shown with reasonable accuracy.

Basic

The design folio includes:
- labelled sketches
- reasonable planning to produce the puppet character
- some understanding of the way that colours or materials have helped to create the puppet character.
- A final design proposal.

Making statements — Advanced

The finished puppet is:
- made to a standard that allows it to work safely, accurately and visually*.

Evaluation shows how these properties have been achieved and how they could have been improved.

Intermediate

The finished puppet:
- is made in a planned manner with care and accuracy evident
- is evaluated to show where faults have occurred and simple changes that could be made to improve some aspects of the finished product.
- Works adequately functionally/visually

Basic

The finished puppet:
- relates to the original design intention
- is made to a functional level of accuracy or appropriate* visual quality
- is evaluated to identify simple changes that could be made to improve an aspect of the finished product.

Key statements are starred (*)

Figure 6.2 RCA assessment guide sheet

This assessment sheet clearly identifies:

- assessment focuses for the project

- success criteria for the project (to be successful . . .)

- success indicators at different levels (basic, intermediate and advanced statements)

(A series of lessons on puppets, from Giffard Park School, is provided in Appendix 6.2, and Appendix 6.3 shows desirable outcomes levels 1–3 of work on puppets.)

Effective assessment and record keeping can be supported by:

- specifying time for observation in a unit of work

- targeting specific pupils for observation and recording in particular lessons, ensuring that all learners are assessed in all subjects over time

- giving responsibility for observation and record keeping to named members of staff in specified lessons

- involving pupils in assessment and recording processes

Sharing objectives with the staff team

Before the lesson discuss with the team:

- how to check for sign of success

- how information about the pupil's understanding and misunderstanding will be communicated during the lesson

The classroom team can then:

- help pupils recognise their own success in each objective

- ensure that success, where possible, is identified, even if it is shown by a single remark or other response

- provide feedback if there is still a lack of understanding so that a different learning approach is tried.

The importance of sharing objectives and success criteria with pupils

Pupils should be clear about what they are expected to learn and what counts as success. Research by the Goldsmith's College Technology Education Research

Unit (TERU) shows that pupils perform for individual teachers in relation to what they think is expected of them. It is important that pupils receive an accurate message as to what is expected. It is even more important that they begin to negotiate their part in defining and achieving these objectives. All adults working with the pupils need to be clear about what is expected of the pupils in a lesson and what counts as success for the members of the group. Pupils who have a positive image of themselves in D&T perform to that image. Assessment and feedback reinforces a pupil's self-image. It is important that pupil's experiences of objectives and success criteria are realistic and positive.

(A useful prompt sheet is provided in Appendix 6.4 on the CD which accompanies this book. There are also stems for writing objectives in Appendix 6.5 and a sample lesson plan in Appendix 6.6.)

How you can share objectives

In the puppets' example you can see how the teacher shares with the pupil's 'to be successful' and includes it in the project booklet introducing the topic. This clearly sets out at the start of a sequence of lessons what will be expected from the pupils. It identifies two clear targets for them (to create an unusual and interesting character and to test their puppet as they design).

In addition, the teacher uses a range of strategies for sharing objectives with pupils and makes sure the objectives are shared and displayed so that Teaching and Support Assistants can refer to them during the lesson, through 'mini plenaries'. The teacher:

- reinforces these two objectives at the beginning of the lesson and, where appropriate, during the lesson in a language that pupils can understand

- agrees the objectives with the pupils as an important aspect of the project: 'What will you learn from making a puppet?' 'What did you learn when we did . . .?'

- displays the objectives in the classroom in a variety of ways – in their written form, with captioned photo cards, and by attaching them to a working display of puppets: 'How could you test this puppet? . . . Pull the strings? . . . Ask a young person to use it? . . . Try out a different colour?'

- links the objectives back to previous relevant work: 'Do you remember when we tested our storybooks to see if young people liked them? How will we test our puppets?'

- uses these objectives as a basis for questioning and feedback in plenaries: 'What is the character of this puppet? What kind of puppet would be sad, scary, kind?

- repeats the objectives during group work and so do the Support Assistants

- gives the pupils short-term targets . . . 'You have 10 minutes to . . .' to help them meet the objectives and maintain focus and engagement

- reviews learning with individuals against the objectives at the end of the lesson

- negotiates targets with pupils at the end of the task/project to inform the objectives for the next design and make assignment

Helping pupils know and recognise the standards they are aiming for

During a designing and making assignment, one way to help pupils to see what is expected of them, is to show them examples of work from previous lessons or other places. But this has to be carefully managed, particularly where pupils lack confidence and think 'I can't do this; I'm no good at this.' Pupils should be shown carefully chosen examples of what others have made with similar abilities rather than work that is beyond them. The examples should be challenging and exciting without being de-motivating. It can help pupils to focus on what is ahead and what they are about to design and make. This is easier to approach if the pupils have had a chance to negotiate what they are designing and making in the first place.

It is also important to show pupils how they are going to get there, the journey of how someone builds up their skills and understanding through focused practical tasks and product evaluation, how they practise and then work further on their project. Pupils should be reassured that they are going to be taught how to do things and supported, so that they know they will be successful.

It can also be helpful to show how some leading designers do not succeed first time, so that they get the feeling that 'we are all learning'.

Involving pupils in peer and self-assessment

As with all pupils, where possible, pupils with learning difficulties should be involved in monitoring their own progress. Pupils need to be encouraged to reflect overtly and in a detailed way on their achievements. Give pupils opportunities to communicate about what they have learned and what they have found difficult. Developing confidence and raising self-esteem are integral parts of this process. Visual records contribute to pupils' sense of achievement – this is reflected well in the pride that pupils take in recording their achievements in their achievement files (see the checklist for the Pasty project as an example of one that a teacher used, to break down the project into small steps that could be ticked off during the lesson, in Appendix 5.1 on the CD that accompanies this book.) Access to the record-keeping system is important if pupils are to be enabled to refer to their targets.

For example, during the design and make project, perhaps towards the end, plan some time to review the activities. Use a visual storyboard of the project pupils are undertaking and together review the pupils' progress towards their D&T targets ('What can you do now that you couldn't do before?'), discuss task 'likes and dislikes' and record comments in an individual planner. Use these to set some targets for the next lessons and record this: 'Next lesson I will . . .'

Encouraging reflection

- Allow sufficient wait time for pupil responses.

- Careful use of questioning helps pupils remember and elaborate on their responses.

- Model how you reflect, for example how you consider alternatives and their implications.

- Encourage pupils to compare this project to previous work. This places heavy demands on memory, where pupils are expected to recall activities and their own performance. Use concrete materials, as well as visual images in the form of photographs, video or computer-generated images, to assist pupils. Thus, using digital pictures and items from the portfolio of a previous project will help.

- Encourage pupils to share opinions with others. Encourage pupils to work/discuss together, focusing on how to improve. Get pupils to show their work to the group and give feedback. Social interaction can be supported through the careful selection of resources and pupil grouping.

Providing effective feedback

Teaching staff and Support Assistants can give feedback to pupils continuously through the lesson. Oral feedback is particularly helpful in D&T as well as written feedback. Ensure that feedback is constructive and focuses on what the pupil has done well, what needs to be done to improve and how to do it. For example, if the pupil is in the middle of making a bag, focus on what processes they have done well (pining, cutting, sewing, accuracy, neatness) and what they need to do next to improve (concentrating carefully when using the sewing machine and controlling it slowly to produce a straight seam).

Remind the pupil of the targets before the learning starts and negotiate the next steps for learning. Use short-term targets to help pupils progress. For example, use the pupil's own designs and products at differing stages of completion to ask the question 'What next?' during a plenary.

Promoting pupil confidence

Build confidence and self-esteem by using small steps to enable pupils to see their own progress. Most stages in designing and making projects can be broken easily into small steps to be rewarded. *For example, in reviewing existing products, pupils can be rewarded for looking at each individual product rather than the set, and perhaps aspects of each individual product (colour, material used, shape).*

Plan projects so that pupils can use previously gained skills in new situations (for example, mixing dough).

Create a secure, supportive environment for pupils to explain their ideas and their thinking.

Recognising progress

For all pupils, including those with learning difficulties, progress is about change and development. For most pupils with learning difficulties, achievements can be predicted and planned for, and progress can be demonstrated in terms of increased knowledge, skills and understanding. Some may follow the same developmental pattern as their fellow pupils, but not necessarily at the same age or rate. Progress may be made in some areas of the curriculum but not in others. For some pupils, progress may be difficult to predict or idiosyncratic and may only be demonstrated in a certain environment with a specific person or materials.

Progress may be recognised when pupils with learning difficulties:

- develop ways to communicate from the use of concrete ways (pointing to materials and tools in front of them they want to use) toward the abstract (using pictures, symbols, print, signs, ICT and the spoken word to ask for materials and tools)

- changing responses to social interactions, from passive co-operation toward active participation with individuals and groups

- needing less support, for example from a helper, from technology, from individualised equipment, in carrying out tasks

- developing a wider range of responses to experiences even if no new skills and knowledge are gained, for example when evaluating products

- increasing their knowledge and understanding about D&T

- maintaining, practising, or combining skills over time and in different situations

- becoming more flexible in learning styles and environments, reducing the need to present activities in consistent and personalised ways

- behaving in a way that does not inhibit learning so frequently

- coping with things that they could not, for example with change or new situations, with trying out new designs, modifying their plans

- choosing not to participate or to respond, for example choosing not to make a particular recipe

The performance descriptions for D&T try to capture some of these elements of progress. Not all pupils will make progress, however. Staff will recognise that, because of their learning difficulties, some pupils may reach a plateau in their achievements, or regress. This is usually temporary, but sometimes can be lengthy or permanent. In such cases, pupils' recorded attainments, or achievements previously predicted by staff, may decline. A slowing of the rate of regression, shown by skills or capabilities being maintained or reactivated, is then a form of progress.

Performance descriptions

Performance descriptions outline early learning and attainment before level 1 in eight levels, from P1 to P8. The performance descriptions can be used by teachers in the same way as the National Curriculum level descriptions to:

- decide which description best fits a pupil's performance over a period of time and in different contexts

- develop or support more focused day-to-day approaches to ongoing teacher assessment by using the descriptions to refine and develop long-, medium- and short-term planning

- track linear progress towards attainment at National Curriculum level 1

- identify lateral progress by looking for related skills at similar levels across their subjects

- record pupils' overall development and achievement, for example at the end of a year or a key stage

Performance descriptions across subjects

The performance descriptions for P1 to P3 are common across all subjects. They outline the types and range of general performance that pupils with learning difficulties might characteristically demonstrate. D&T examples are included to illustrate some of the ways in which staff might identify attainment in different subject contexts.

PERFORMANCE DESCRIPTIONS IN D&T, P1–P3

P1 (i) Pupils encounter activities and experiences. They may be passive or resistant. They may show simple reflex responses, *for example, startling at sudden noises or movements.* Any participation is fully prompted.

P1 (ii) Pupils show emerging awareness of activities and experiences. They may have periods when they appear alert and ready to focus their attention on certain people, events, objects or parts of objects, *for example, pausing over food smells in the room.* They may give intermittent reactions, *for example, sometimes briefly grasping materials placed in their hands.*

P2 (i) Pupils begin to respond consistently to familiar people, events and objects. They react to new activities and experiences, *for example, turning to a particular food item.* They begin to show interest in people, events and objects, *for example, briefly focusing on the sound of a making activity.* They accept and engage in coactive exploration, *for example, with staff support, feeling the textures of wood, metal, plastic, fabric and foods.*

P2 (ii) Pupils begin to be proactive in their interactions. They communicate consistent preferences and affective responses, *for example, turning towards a particular food item or colour product.* They recognise familiar people, events and objects, *for example, grasping the handle of a tool.* They perform actions, often by trial and improvement, and they remember learned responses over short periods of time, *for example, lifting and lowering a tool or pressing their fingers into soft dough several times.* They cooperate with shared exploration and supported participation, *for example, working with an adult to apply glue to a surface.*

P3 (i) Pupils begin to communicate intentionally. They seek attention through eye contact, gesture or action. They request events or activities, *for example, reaching out towards a particular piece of equipment.* They participate in shared activities with less support. They sustain concentration for short periods. They explore materials in increasingly complex ways, *for example, tearing, squashing, mixing or bending materials.* They observe the results of their own actions with interest, *for example, after bending sheet materials.* They remember learned responses over more extended periods, *for example, banging with a hammer.*

P3 (ii) Pupils use emerging conventional communication. They greet known people and may initiate interactions and activities, *for example, pushing the spoon into the mixing bowl.* They can remember learned responses over increasing periods of time and may anticipate known events, *for example, covering their ears before a loud sound.* They may respond to options and choices with actions or gestures, *for example, picking up one tool rather than another.* They actively explore objects and events for more extended periods, *for example, banging, scraping, rubbing or pressing tools against a surface.* They apply potential solutions systematically to problems, *for example, pressing materials together.*

PERFORMANCE DESCRIPTIONS IN DESIGN AND TECHNOLOGY, P4–P8

From level P4 to P8, many believe it is possible to describe pupils' performance in a way that indicates the emergence of skills, knowledge and understanding in D&T. The descriptions provide an example of how this can be done.

P4 With help, pupils begin to assemble components provided for an activity, *for example, placing bricks together.* They contribute to activities by coactively grasping and moving simple tools, *for example, a glue spreader.* They explore options within a limited range of materials, *for example, adding grapes or chopped apple to a fruit salad.*

P5 Pupils use a basic tool, with support, *for example, pushing a roller.* They demonstrate preferences for products, materials and ingredients, *for example, selecting a preferred filling for a sandwich.*

P6 Pupils recognise familiar products and explore the different parts they are made from. They watch others using a basic tool and copy the actions, *for example, preparing a surface with a glass paper block.* They begin to offer responses to making activities, *for example, suggesting the colour or shape of a product.*

P7 Pupils operate familiar products, with support, and explore how they work. They use basic tools or equipment in simple processes, chosen in negotiation with staff, *for example, in cutting or shaping materials.* They begin to communicate preferences in their designing and making, *for example, adding selected felt shapes to fabric.*

P8 Pupils explore familiar products and communicate views about them when prompted. With help, they manipulate a wider range of basic tools in making activities, *for example, joining components together to make their intended product.* They begin to contribute to decisions about what they will do and how, *for example, communicating their approval of certain features of a process.*

Examples

The following examples show how both the general descriptions of attainment at levels P1 to P3 and the subject-focused descriptions at P4 to P8 can be used in curriculum plans to structure learning. Using plans like these, staff and pupils can anticipate pupil responses, note and record them, and then build on them to promote learning.

Puppets/Joseph's coat project – Indicative P level 4

Amanda was able to select a garment she wanted to wear. She was able to select from a choice of two fabrics for dressing a doll for a party context. She was able to draw a repeating pattern by being given one crayon at a time, e.g. red then blue, then red, etc. Amanda could select dye colour for batik patterns and was able to perform threading action with laces. With help, she could use a lace to join together the fabric pieces she had selected. She was able to select buttons and sequins but needed help in attaching them to her garment. Her comment on her finished garment was 'nice'.

Amanda's work is indicative of a pupil working at level P4.

Snack Bar project – Indicative P level 6

Jack is a Year 7 boy, who has severe learning difficulties and epilepsy as a result of serious illness when he was a young child. In design and technology, he finds it difficult to record designs and plan his own work and needs much adult encouragement to participate actively in lessons. Jack can communicate using three or four word phrases; he is just learning to copy write and he is at an early reading stage. In this project, Jack had to try to give his opinion about the different snack bars and make choices to develop a healthy recipe from given ingredients.

Jack was not keen to taste or give opinions about the commercially produced snack bars, but with encouragement would indicate which of them he had tried. He worked in a small group to experience following recipes (with symbols) with staff help and, with much encouragement, made his own choice between cake-based and biscuit-based snack bars. He practised putting foods into the three traffic light groups.

Jack chose his additions to his plain cake-based snack bar recipe (with muesli) and made it with adult assistance. Jack could copy the actions of the assistant. He said his choice was 'good' when asked.

He enjoyed the experiments with different wrapping materials and chose a suitable material to wrap his bar. Jack was helped to ring his choices on his worksheets to which symbols were added to aid his understanding.

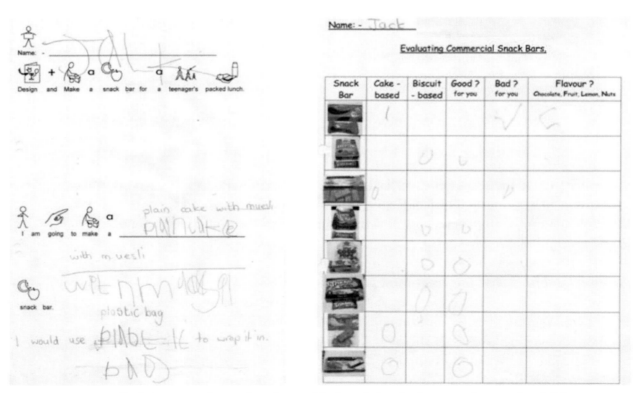

Jack is currently performing at National Curriculum attainment level P6.

Puppets project – Indicative P level 8

Lewis decided his plate puppet would be of a man. He discussed his ideas and considered both people he knew and characters in books. His ideas developed during discussions and while looking at the materials available to him. He was able to communicate his ideas by producing a labelled diagram on a proforma design sheet.

During the making phase, Lewis demonstrated that he was able to select appropriate tools and materials, and mark out, cut and shape the materials. He was also able to assemble the components.

Evaluation was ongoing, during which Lewis was able to talk about his ideas. On completion of the product, Lewis was able to say what he liked and disliked, but was not able to identify ways in which he could improve his work in the future.

Lewis' finished product is characteristic of a child working at level P8, but he was able to demonstrate some characteristics of level 1 during the design phase.

(A scheme of work plan is included for this work in Appendix 6.2 on the CD which accompanies this book.)

Using performance descriptions to recognise attainment

Assessment needs to be viewed in its widest sense – it is not just about marking. Making regular and frequent checks on pupils' acquisition of knowledge, understanding and skills is essential in order to judge pace and progression. What is required is the building up and recording of a range of evidence on which teacher judgements can be based. Such evidence can be gained through observation of pupils while they are working on tasks, combined with folder work, products and information gained while talking to the pupil. Pupils with learning difficulties often produce very little written or supporting evidence for their work. They find it difficult to record their thoughts and design decisions. If the teacher looks only at the folder and the end product made by the pupil they are often faced with evidence that reveals little of the actual quality of design thinking or depth of knowledge held by the pupil.

QCA (www.qca.org.uk) have developed a framework for recognising attainment. It is not intended as a tool to measure hierarchical and linear progress mechanistically from encounter to attainment, but it may give teachers a greater understanding of how pupils move through a learning process. Teachers may wish to use this framework to develop their own assessment tools so they take into account the differing needs of their pupils across the curriculum.

> **A FRAMEWORK FOR RECOGNISING ATTAINMENT**
>
> **Encounter**
> Pupils are present during an experience or activity without any obvious learning outcome, although for some pupils, *for example, those who withhold their attention or their presence from many situations, their willingness to tolerate a shared activity may, in itself, be significant.*
>
> **Awareness**
> Pupils appear to show awareness that something has happened and notice, fleetingly focus on or attend to an object, event or person, *for example, by briefly interrupting a pattern of self-absorbed movement or vocalisation.*
>
> **Attention and response**
> Pupils attend and begin to respond, often not consistently, to what is happening, *for example, by showing signs of surprise, enjoyment, frustration or dissatisfaction, demonstrating the beginning of an ability to distinguish between different people, objects, events and places.*
>
> **Engagement**
> Pupils show more consistent attention to, and can tell the difference between, specific events in their surroundings, *for example, by focused looking or listening; turning to locate objects, events or people; following moving objects and events through movements of their eyes, head or other body parts.*
>
> **Participation**
> Pupils engage in sharing, taking turns and the anticipation of familiar sequences of events, *for example, by smiling, vocalising or showing other signs of excitement, although these responses may be supported by staff or other pupils.*
>
> **Involvement**
> Pupils actively strive to reach out, join in or comment in some way on the activity itself or on the actions or responses of the other pupils, *for example, by making exploratory hand and arm movements, seeking eye contact with staff or other pupils, or by speaking, signing or gesturing.*
>
> **Gaining skills**
> Pupils gain, strengthen or make general use of their skills, and understanding knowledge, concepts or understanding that relate to their experience of the curriculum, *for example, they can recognise the features of an object and understand its relevance, significance and use.*

What records do you need to keep?

Keeping up-to-date records can help staff with their future planning. Records can show what pupils know and can do, what teaching methods have worked well and what affects the pupil's performance, such as health or a change in home circumstances.

For pupils with learning difficulties, records of experiences, progress and achievements in relation to targets in their IEPs and curriculum plans should focus on significant responses or ways of learning. A system should be flexible enough to include unexpected or unusual responses, however these occur. The needs of individual pupils may determine the type of record, and it may be necessary to draw up individual standards.

It is up to staff to decide the kinds of records they keep. Their decision will be based on how useful they and other staff find the records. Records may include:

- extracts from curriculum plans (as records of experience)

- comments about pupil responses

- annotated samples of work

- photographs, or tape or video sequences

- pupil self-assessment and peer recordings

- a pupil's record of achievement or progress file

- assessments related to external accreditation

Regular monitoring and recording of pupils' responses and progress identifies areas where pupils are making steady progress and where progress is not being maintained. The responses of some pupils may change from lesson to lesson and topic to topic and may be dependent on factors such as:

- preferences for certain helpers

- grouping or positioning with certain pupils

- different environments

- the time of day

- access to favourite tools/equipment

- particular sorts of sensory experience, for example tasting, mixing dough, touching products

- focus material being used, for example plastic, food, metal

- emerging talents in particular aspects of designing and making

Accreditation at Key Stage 4

Sir Ron Dearing, in his *Review of Qualifications for 16–19 year olds* recommended the development of qualifications at Entry level. The intention was to 'encourage and recognise achievement by a wider range of learners than at present'. The introduction of Entry level has meant that people with a lower level of learning are now able to gain nationally recognised qualifications.

Pupils who are not able to obtain full GCSE credit can be given the option of following an Entry Level Certificate as offered by awarding bodies such as AQA, WJEC and OCR. Certificates are based on the Design and Technology National

Curriculum Order and were designed to record the achievements of pupils who are unlikely to manage a GCSE grade A*–G. This allows these pupils to follow the same scheme of work as GCSE pupils so that all can be taught in the same class.

As with the GCSE syllabus, a Certificate course provides opportunities for pupils to develop an awareness of the nature and significance of D&T in a rapidly changing society, and to do so with an approach based in designing and making in a particular focus area (textiles, food, resistant materials). The syllabuses offer a system of assessment which recognises the need for greater teacher involvement in candidates with SEN work, and which is based on clear targets and a coherent set of criteria for rewarding positive achievement.

What is Entry level?

Entry level is the first level of the national qualifications framework. It lies beneath Foundation level and is divided into three sublevels: 1, 2 and 3, with 3 being the highest. These sublevels are broadly comparable with National Curriculum levels 1, 2 and 3. Many certificates are made up of a number of units. Each unit is assessed separately so that pupils' small steps of achievement can be recognised on the way to completing the full certificate.

There are no rules about which units, or how many, must be included in a certificate. This means awarding bodies can create certificates that meet the diverse needs of learners at this level. The units can also be at one or more of the entry sublevels (1, 2 or 3) if it is appropriate. Since there is no single structure and no standard amount of content or number of units, courses for Entry Level Certificates do not have to be completed within a set time limit. Pupils working at this level tend to make progress at varying speeds, so different pupils may complete the same certificate at very different rates. In practice, courses run in schools leading to Entry Level Certificates in National Curriculum subjects are usually set up as one- or two-year programmes, spanning Years 10 and 11.

At least 50% of D&T Entry Level Certificate is assessed 'externally', that is through tests, assignments or tasks that are:

- set and marked by the awarding body

- set by the awarding body, marked by the centre and moderated by the awarding body

- designed by the centre, validated before they are used by the awarding body, marked by the centre and moderated by the awarding body

These tests, assignments and tasks can be practical, written or oral. The remainder of the certificate is assessed 'internally', that is by teachers in the pupil's centre. Often pupils compile a portfolio showing evidence of their achievement. The evidence can be in a range of forms such as witness statements, video, audio and photographs.

Awarding bodies can provide more information about Entry level. Visit individual awarding body websites for more information. A list of these websites is to be found in Appendix 6.7 on the CD which accompanies this book.

Summary

- Be clear about what learning outcomes are expected from the activity. Assessment is easier if pupils know what they are meant to show evidence of, and teachers know what they are looking for.

- Try to use as many different assessment methods as possible – accessing written, drawn, spoken and practical evidence. Some evidence of learning can be written or pictorial, but other evidence arises while pupils are discussing or answering questions. Talk to the pupil and question them as this may reveal a more thorough understanding than their written work suggests. Annotations on pupils' work and notes in the teacher's mark book are an effective way of recording this evidence. If you write the results of the discussion on the pupil's work, this will provide a permanent record and give the pupil a model to help them to know what to write next time. Pupil diaries and review sheets are also useful.

- Assessment should always be positive, acknowledging what has been achieved against set targets rather than making comparisons with the achievements of others. Effective assessment means ensuring that pupils are rewarded for what they know, understand and can do.

- Assessment should be used to give pupils feedback about their work and their learning and to encourage them to assess their own progress, with both teachers and other pupils reviewing what has been achieved and thinking about next steps.

- Recognise and report as many different aspects as possible.

- Sensitive observation and diagnostic tests will help to pinpoint areas of weakness in a subject which may have been missed by the pupil and which requires extra attention. They also help to identify strengths on which the teacher can build.

Managing Support

The ultimate responsibility for a pupil's access to the D&T curriculum is that of the classroom teacher. Support staff facilitate the delivery of an appropriately differentiated curriculum under the direction of the D&T teacher. (Appendix 7.1 on the CD that accompanies this book gives advice on how to make the most of your support staff.)

> Design and technology is a practical subject, one which encourages children to think and do, to try out and reflect. This type of activity can be very time consuming for teachers and therefore extra help is often welcomed in the classroom.
>
> (*A Guide for Teacher Assistants*, Design and Technology Association 1996)

D&T teachers and support staff working together

If you are going to be working together on a regular basis, the D&T teacher should:

- Give the support staff clear instructions for specific tasks.

- Provide guidance on how to carry out tasks.

You should share the:

- school's policy for D&T

- the correct way of using tools and equipment

- health and safety guidelines

- where to find materials, tools and equipment

- where to find other resources for D&T

- practical classroom routines

(The planning and monitoring grids – weekly planning grid, daily planning grid, weekly support notes and individual support records – supplied in Appendix 7 on the CD which accompanies this book can help you plan and record the support simply.)

Tips for the teacher on working with support staff

- Direct the support staff and give them clear instructions.

- Explain the dos and don'ts of how you work right from the start.

- Find out about their particular interests and areas of expertise (for example, food, textiles, sketching, ICT).

- Be clear about the skills and knowledge they may need to develop and how to support them, for example basic food hygiene, machine skills.

- Ask them if they have any concerns.

Tips for the support staff on working with the teacher

- Find out what is expected of you.

- Ask if you are not sure of something.

- Don't intrude or take over – remember you are working under the teacher's direction.

- Arrive early to allow time to speak to the teacher and set up resources.

- Be discreet – information about individual children should be treated as confidential.

- Give feedback that might be useful to the teacher.

- Be prepared to learn new things.

Supporting designing and making in D&T

Lessons in D&T will probably involve a Support Assistant in:

- showing children how to do something

- talking to children while they are working

- supporting practical work

Sometimes, they are also asked to supervise group work, organise and maintain resources and create displays to support learning.

Showing children how to do something

One frequent task will be demonstrating how to do something to a small group or individual. Perhaps the teacher will demonstrate to the whole class and you will be reinforcing by repeating that as required. Perhaps you will be showing the child you are supporting a specific technique or skill, such as cutting, joining, mixing or using a piece of equipment, such as threading a sewing machine.

Preparing for demonstrations

- Think about what you are going to do and say in advance.

- Practise the technique until you are confident yourself – teachers often do this.

- Break down the process into smaller stages.

- Think about the possible tricky points for pupils – for example, holding the equipment the right way.

- Choose the most important points to tell pupils. How will you help them remember?

- Plan some questions.

- Find out if there are any health and safety issues.

- Have the equipment and materials ready and well laid out.

When you are demonstrating

- Demonstrations are interactive, not one-way dialogues.

- Keep the group size small.

- Position yourself so that everyone can see, that they can sit or stand comfortably and not get distracted.

- Explain each step clearly and simply as you demonstrate. You are modelling good technique.

- Work much more slowly than usual; provide a running commentary to point out the detail of each stage.

- Reinforce the important points. Repeat your points and try to explain why things are done in a particular way. Emphasise points by drawing pupils' attention to them . . . 'Do you see how this . . . ?' Pause and let the pupils look.

- Make sure the pupils pay attention, involve them by asking questions, make them touch, handle, look, smell, listen . . . to get a better understanding (for example, if mixing dough and you wish to reinforce the point about how wet/dry it will be).

- Keep eye contact with the group and check they understand. Involve them if you can, for example by holding things, measuring, choosing.

- Recap on what you have done at the end. If they are going to carry out the task immediately make sure they all know the first couple of steps.

Talking to pupils while they are designing and making

One of the real benefits of this practical subject is the opportunity Support Assistants get to talk to pupils as they work through their tasks. Much of this talking seems informal chatting but it can make a significant contribution to their learning, particularly for those pupils who find it hard to speak up in whole-class situations. Talking to pupils, intervening with questions, providing praise and encouragement, and asking their opinions make a real difference to pupils' learning and success.

Questions you can ask pupils

Well-designed questions lead pupils from unsorted knowledge to organised understanding. Questioning is an area that is characterised by a great deal of instinctive practice; such questions allow you to reflect on, analyse and develop the effectiveness of what you do. Effective questioning is not just a matter of planning which questions to ask, but also planning to stage or sequence those questions so that they guide the pupils toward key lesson objectives. Questioning pupils with SEN should be done in an atmosphere where pupils feel secure enough to take risks and be tentative. Try to allow thinking time, use wait time and value all answers given. Give credit for trying, and maintain positive eye contact and body language to encourage pupils.

The wording of questions becomes acutely important when working with pupils with learning difficulties. Avoid questions such as, 'Can you explain . . .?', 'Are you able to describe . . . ?' Pupils with special educational needs may interpret them literally and answer yes/no. Replace them with, 'Explain to me', 'Describe to me . . .'. Avoid negative phrases such as, 'I'm not clear about . . .' Use 'Tell me what you mean . . .'

It is helpful to refer to one pupil's answer to another pupil to generate discussion. Encourage pupils to answer each other's questions: 'What do you think about that?' Encourage them to add to and challenge the answers provided by others. They should listen to each other's questions and answers as well as yours. This develops confidence, social interaction and co-operative working.

Looking at existing products

One activity required by the National Curriculum is to investigate and evaluate existing products to inform and explore new design ideas. Looking at existing products is a rich source of talking and questioning. Don't be afraid to express an opinion or share your experiences which might be relevant to what the pupils are doing: 'They have just started recycling bottles and glasses in my area, I think it's a good idea because . . .'; 'I tried a new bread from the supermarket this week. It had apricots and walnuts in it, and that gave it an interesting flavour . . .'

When thinking about questions for product evaluation:

- Show pupils how to formulate their own questions, for example from a list provided: 'What questions could we ask about this product?'

- Ask pupils how they feel about the product and for their opinions to build their self-esteem.

- Have groups working on different sets of questions – match the level of challenge to the ability to move different pupils forward.

- Plan higher order questions where appropriate – moving pupils from factual recall and comprehension to application, analysis, synthesis and evaluation.

Knowledge – factual, recall and recognition

Describe the product:

- What is it made from?

- Who is it for?

- When would it be used?

- Where is it used?

- How often is it used?

- Which one . . .?

- What is the best one for doing . . .?

- How much does it cost?

- Where is it sold?

- Who designed and made this?

- How has it been made?

- Where is it from?

- What sort/type/category of product is it?

- What other products are like this?

Comprehension – translating, interpreting and extrapolating

- Do I like it?

- Is it what I need?

- Is it the right size, shape, pattern, colour, smell, taste?

- Is it safe?

- Does it do the intended job?

- Is it value for money?

- What does it cost in relation to the income of the potential users?

- Demonstrate how the product is used.

- Explain why this product was developed.

- Explain what is meant by . . . (label or product feature)

- Give an example of . . .

- Is this the same as . . . ?

- What would happen if this product was used for . . . (another purpose)?

Application – to situations that are new/new slants

- What is my reaction to this product?

- Who might the owner be?

- Why might they want to buy it?

- Does it work well?

- What ingredients and processes have been used – why?

- Does it do what it was intended to?

- Does it look and taste good?

- How well is it made?

- Is it nicely finished?

- Is the cost appropriate?

- Is it really needed?

- How much will this product change people's lives?

- Choose the best statements that apply to this product (statements given).

- How is it promoted and packaged?

- Predict what would happen if . . .

Analysis – breaking down into parts/forms

- What is the function of this product/parts of the product?

- What do people think of this product?

- Does everyone think this product is a good invention?

- Who is it for?

- What assumptions have been made about the people who might use it?

- Whose needs or wants were possibly considered during designing and making this product?

- Why is this product like this?

- What are the motives of the people who design and make it?

- What is the relationship between this product and . . .?

- What makes this product distinct from others of its type?

- Does this product have an identity or image?

- How has this been achieved?

- Does the promotion target a particular age group or group of people?

- What are they trying to say about the product?

- How are they persuading you?

- What do people believe about this product – is it true?

Synthesis – combining elements into a pattern not clearly there before

- Would I want to own or use it?

- What would this reveal about me?

- What influenced the appearance and the way it works?

- How might the design have been developed?

- How would you test this to see . . .?

- Propose an alternative solution to the product or part of product.

- How else would you . . .?

- Suggest changes you could make to . . .

- Develop a list of important features.

- How is this product different from one from five years ago/another culture?

- How will this product be different in ten years' time?

- What would happen if you were to add . . .?

- What would happen if you were to make it?

- Why did the designer make it this way?

- What happens to it after use? How long will it last?

Evaluation – according to criteria and state reasons

- What effect will this product have on people's lives and relationships?
- Is this a better product than . . .?
- Is this a more important invention than . . .?
- Is this a more appropriate solution than . . .?
- What is wrong with this product?
- Why is this product not as popular as . . .?
- What could be done better or differently?
- How good is this product compared to . . .?
- What difficulties do users find with this product?
- What difficulties do manufacturers have making this product?
- What negative impacts does this product have on other people?
- Why have these particular ingredients been chosen?
- Can it be part of a sustainable world?
- Where do the ingredients come from?
- Is there a problem with side effects?
- What else could have been used?

Questions to ask to get pupils organised

Encourage pupils to think for themselves. Support Assistants should promote independence at all times. Ask questions that encourage pupils to think about what they are doing. Probe for explanation and justification by using further questions to extend thinking that requires more than a one-word answer: 'Explain . . . ?', 'Why . . . ?', 'What makes you think that?', 'What would happen if . . .?', 'Tell me more . . .'

- What do you need to do first?
- What will you need?
- Where are you going to work?
- Who will you work with?
- Who is doing what in your group?
- How long have you got to do this task?

Questions to help when designing

Sometimes, pupils find designing difficult and will need support and feedback to keep them on task. Don't talk to them too much! Try to balance asking the right questions against talking so much that it distracts the pupils from what they are trying to do, or prevents them from sorting things out for themselves. But help pupils to move forward by intervening with more open questions that have more than one answer and require extended responses. Use speculative 'What if' questions. Use 'Why?' as the opening to questions.

Avoid making decisions for the pupil. Give them opportunities to make choices and decisions themselves. Encourage independent behaviour.

Reinforce the use of key technical vocabulary, such as 'ideas', 'model', 'user', 'purpose', 'design criteria'. Sometimes it will be helpful to simplify the language that is used, and to help pupils by recording their answers and designs for them or with them. They should still retain ownership of the work.

- Who is it for?

- What do they need?

- What do you want to find out?

- How will they use it?

- What else is like this?

- What did your research tell you?

- What size does it need to be?

- What else could you use?

- What else would work?

- What would happen if you . . .?

- How are you going to make it?

- How could you try it out before you make it . . . or model it?

- How could you . . .?

- What do we call it when we . . .?

Questions to help when making

In practical lessons when the pupil needs to manipulate specialised equipment, the Support Assistant should work *under the direction of the pupils*. Thus questions will often be, 'What would you like me to do first?'

Where pupils are able to work more independently, listen carefully to pupils' answers: it will tell you whether they understand and are able to get on with the task. Use questions to develop self-help skills. Avoid creating dependency. Intervene to reinforce key points and make learning explicit for pupils: 'Why do we use oven gloves to take out the tray?' (instructions); 'Why do you like the green one?' (opinions); 'I think that you have sewn that very carefully' (feedback); 'Do you think you will need to add some more water?' (advice); 'Don't forget to . . .' (reminder); 'Look at the way this is glued together' (pointing out); 'What do we call this kind of joint?' (reinforcing technical vocabulary).

- What tool would be best for that job?

- How are you going to join those pieces together?

- What could you use?

- How could you make those the right size?

- How are you going to decorate it/finish it?

- How could you make that part look better?

Supporting practical work

A high proportion of time in D&T lessons is practical work, and Support Assistants play an important role here in preparing materials, demonstrating how to do something and talking to children while they are working. Watching and listening will be very important – it will help you to identify what is really going on, how much help individuals need and what kind of help is appropriate.

D&T is about developing pupils' ability to design and make things by themselves, so don't carry out tasks for them, unless this has been deemed appropriate. The Support Assistant's role is to facilitate independent learning and to enable the pupils to do as much as possible for him/herself. Pupils who lack self-confidence will sometimes plead with you to do it for them. Don't! Guide pupils by talking them through the task, or allow them to instruct you so that you carry out tasks on their behalf. They will need more support if they are doing something for the first time.

Often it will be helpful to break down the task into smaller steps, to simplify the language used in the work, and keep the pupil on task with feedback and prompting.

Working alongside the teacher in practical lessons

- Ask the teacher if the practical activity needs to be adapted for the pupil you are supporting, for example if there is special equipment you can use.

- Reinforce the classroom routines for setting up work and clearing away.

- Don't do things for pupils that they can do themselves, for example clearing up.

- Labelling cupboards with a digital photo/name label helps pupils to access the equipment they need independently.

- Encourage the pupil to remember where resources are kept.

- Remind them how to work safely and hygienically.

- Encourage them to work tidily.

- Encourage them to work accurately.

- Observe their posture, position and handling of equipment, and correct where needed.

- Ensure the class has equal access to materials and equipment.

- Use the correct names for tools and equipment, and processes to reinforce key vocabulary.

Helping support staff learn about D&T so that they can support effectively

D&T is a dynamic subject, and teachers constantly update their knowledge and skills to keep abreast of the breadth of the subject and the new developments within it. Support Assistants similarly will have different strengths and requirements for professional development.

Case study

Katrina, a Support Assistant, was working in food technology lessons supporting a pupil with cognitive and learning difficulties. She did not feel confident in her understanding about food safety and hygiene in practical classrooms and used the British Nutrition Foundation CD *Teaching Food Safety* as a distance learning tool. This is an interactive learning programme aimed at teachers training to teach food technology. After answering a series of quiz questions, she worked through a set of training modules to bring her knowledge up to date. The section on setting up food activities in the classroom and safe food handling were particularly helpful.

Case study

Jack, a Support Assistant, joined a D&T team training day on ICT in D&T, so that he was familiar with the latest CAD/CAM software that the pupils were using (for example, Prodesktop, Speedstep and Crocodile Clips). Jack learned how the software can be used for designing and making. He then discussed with the staff how to support pupils with learning difficulties when they are using ICT.

Summary

Support Assistants are a rich resource when used effectively and they can be invaluable to the pressed D&T teacher. They often enjoy supporting design and technology lessons because the practical nature of the subject makes it easy to join in a classroom situation and provide individual support to those who need it, relatively inconspicuously.

Specialist support may be useful for:

- simplifying the language used in the work

- presenting the project in smaller steps and guiding the pupil through

- keeping the student on task with support and feedback

- writing and recording for the student

- helping the pupil with specialist equipment

- helping with personal organisation or with physical or medical needs

Support Assistants are used most effectively where:

- Careful consideration has been given to where the help could be used best.

- The teacher and the support staff are able to discuss and plan strategies for working together.

- The pupil is clear about why the extra help is given.

- The support staff are involved in feedback and assessment of the pupil's work.

CHAPTER 8

Real Pupils in Real Classrooms

This chapter introduces some case studies of pupils and the strategies their D&T teachers use to support them in gaining the fullest possible D&T curriculum for their needs. You may like to use these case studies as a reference point or to assist you during INSET sessions with your department.

INSET – SPECIAL CONTRIBUTIONS FROM D&T IN YOUR SCHOOL

- What special contributions do you look for from D&T to balance the curriculum for your pupils with SEN?
- How can you further promote the value of D&T for pupils with special educational needs to your colleagues, and parents? Review (stand back as an outsider) how others perceive the nature of the work and achievements by pupils with SEN in D&T.
- Consider the range of SEN you experience across your school and the problems these may present for students' learning in design and technology. What solutions and support can you offer?

Case studies

The case studies that follow introduce:

- Kuli in Year 8 with hearing impairment

- Harry in Year 7 with dyslexia

- Megan in Year 10 who uses a wheelchair

- Steven in Year 9 with emotional, behavioural and social difficulties

- Matthew in Year 9 with cognitive and learning difficulties

- Bhavini in Year 9 who is visually impaired

- Susan in Year 10 who has complex difficulties, including Autistic Spectrum Disorder

- Jenny in Year 7 who has Down's Syndrome

Kuli

Kuli has significant hearing loss. He has some hearing in his right ear but is heavily reliant on his hearing aid and visual cues ranging from lip reading to studying body language and facial expression to get the gist and tone of what people are saying. He often misses crucial details. Reading is a useful alternative input and his mechanical reading skills are good, but he does not always get the full message because of language delay. He has problems with new vocabulary and with asking and responding to questions.

Now in Year 8, he follows the same timetable as the rest of his class for most of the week but he has some individual tutorial sessions with a teacher of the deaf to help with his understanding of the curriculum and to focus on his speech and language development. This is essential, but it does mean that he misses some classes, so he is not always up to speed with a subject

He has a good sense of humour but appreciates visual jokes more than ones which are language based. He is very literal and is puzzled by all sorts of idioms. He was shocked when he heard that someone had been 'painting the town red' as he thought this was an act of vandalism! Even when he knows what he wants to say he does not always have the words or structures to communicate accurately what he knows.

Everyone is very pleasant and quite friendly to him but he is not really part of any group and quite often misunderstands what other kids are saying. He has a Support Assistant which again marks him out as different. He gets quite frustrated because he always has ideas that are too complex for his expressive ability. He can be very sulky and has temper tantrums.

Strategies

- Kuli needs to know what is coming up in the next few lessons so he can prepare the vocabulary and get some sense of the main concepts so he can follow what is being said.

- A good Support Assistant will find ways of displaying information visually, using drawings, pictures, signs, symbols, sign language, mime, animations on the computer, etc.

- Make sure demonstrations and explanations are seen and understood.

- Try to reduce the general hum of noise in the classroom, particularly during practical lessons.

- Present one source of information at a time: it is hard for him to focus on what you are saying at the same time as looking at a book or watching what you are writing on a board.

- Phrase questions carefully and always say his name beforehand.

Project Example – Alarms

The teacher introduced a task that he felt would engage the interest of all of the pupils: to design and manufacture alarms that could be used in a real-life situation.

The teacher told the pupils that they could chose their own inputs and outputs for the alarm, and asked them to decide for themselves on a purpose for their alarm. The added bonus of this project for Kuli was that the teacher suggested it would be good if he were able to make an alarm for people in his situation with significant hearing loss. This motivated him a lot.

Kuli had to develop a specification for his product by examining existing alarms and referring to his own proposals. At this point, the teacher was careful to check Kuli's understanding by posing focused questions. Kuli decided to make a plant dryness indicator. When the soil around the plant becomes dry, the light-emitting diode (LED) is activated.

The pupils used a systems and control simulator program to help them start the project. Next, the teacher gave the class a generic printed circuit board so that they could insert their own inputs and outputs. Kuli found it helpful to use a larger PCB that had wide tracks and pads. In the following lessons, the pupils added components to their PCBs and learnt how to use a multi-meter to check soldering. The teacher provided differentiated worksheets to support Kuli during the manufacturing processes. He ensured that he gave specific feedback to Kuli as his ideas developed.

As the pupils had used a generic PCB, this meant that they did not have to manufacture individual circuit boards and spent only a small amount of time on fault finding. This freed up more lesson time to concentrate on the designing.

The teacher thought of ways to help grab the pupils' interest. For example, when he gave them the task of designing casings he decided to allow them to choose whichever medium they felt most confident working with. He suggested they could, for example, make models in card, or through using CAD or traditional graphics techniques.

The teacher had set up this project so that the pupils could carry out the designing and making activity within a defined framework while also having the freedom to design something they would find most useful. He noticed that this increased motivation in Kuli and others in the class. It allowed the pupils to demonstrate their own ideas both to the teacher and to each other. This gave Kuli the confidence to work on his own initiative and helped secure his motivation and concentration.

Harry

Harry is a very anxious little boy and, although he has now started at secondary school, he still seems to be a 'little boy'. His parents have been very concerned about his slow progress in reading and writing and arranged for a dyslexia assessment when he was eight years old. They also employ a private tutor who comes to the house for two hours per week and they spend time each evening and at weekends hearing him read and working on phonics with him.

Harry expresses himself well orally using words which are very sophisticated and adult. His reading is improving (RA 8.4) but his handwriting and spelling are so poor that it is sometimes difficult to work out what he has written. He doesn't just confuse *b* and *d* but also *h* and *y*, *p* and *b*. Increasingly, he uses a small bank of words that he knows he can spell.

His parents want him to be withdrawn from French on the grounds that he has enough problems with English. The French teacher reports that Harry is doing well with his comprehension and spoken French, and is one of the more able children in the class.

Some staff get exasperated with Harry as he is quite clumsy, seems to be in a dream half the time and cannot remember a simple sequence of instructions. He has difficulty telling left from right and so is often talking about the wrong diagram in a book or out of step in PE and sport. 'He's just not trying,' said one teacher, while others think he needs 'to grow up a bit.'

He is popular with the girls in his class and recently has made friends with some of the boys in the choir. Music is Harry's great passion, but his parents are not willing for him to learn an instrument at the moment.

Strategies

- Staff to talk to the parents about Harry's lack of confidence.

- Provide Harry with strategies for distinguishing left from right.

- Find out how he has learnt things and see if similar strategies would work in the classroom.

- Investigate the possibility of using a computer with spellchecker at home and school to cope with orthographic and spelling difficulties.

- Offer lots of praise.

- Allow more time for practical work if needed.

- Focus on Harry's strengths – talk about and discuss designs, products, making and evaluating rather than writing about them.

- Make use of pictures, plans, flowcharts, visual instruction sheets with digital images of processes.

- Provide templates to fill in and key words to use.

- Practise names of equipment and processes to reinforce key vocabulary.

- Show Harry how to annotate neatly.

Project example – Design and make a snack bar

The teacher set Harry a design and make assignment that required him to think about how a food product is created, see how a recipe can be altered to suit different tastes, and to learn how important nutritional content is.

Luckily, Harry enjoys the practical aspects of design and technology: the reading and writing have a real purpose in the lesson as they lead to making something edible! Harry enjoys the success of seeing something he has made and this has given him confidence to record his ideas and evaluations in a simple way.

Through group discussion and teacher-led prompts, Harry was encouraged to devise three criteria against which to evaluate his product:

- taste good

- 'do you good'

- well wrapped to travel in a lunch box

The teacher provided a range of commercially produced snack bars for the groups to unwrap, examine, discuss, taste and evaluate nutritionally and against the set criteria for the product. It was more important to discuss and describe the products than record at this point, and the teacher frequently praised Harry for his contributions. Harry was given a chart template to fill in the information collected and a simple word bank to use in doing it.

The teacher talked about the nutritional value of foods – classifying the food groups and the balanced plate, healthy-eating model. He was assisted in putting examples of foods into the right section of the plate by a Support Assistant.

During the focused practical tasks, Harry was shown how to make both biscuit and cake-based products and how to add a given variety of ingredients to alter the taste and nutritional content of the product. Harry practised naming and weighing ingredients, using a variety of equipment, including electrically driven, hand food mixers. He tried different 'toppings' and decoration on the snack bars. The teacher asked him to use matching cards to show the sequence of actions after he had made the recipe.

The teacher devised a chart to simplify Harry's choice of ingredients and he cooked his design. He had to focus on the steps in the recipe, and the teacher supported him, making sure he was doing one step at a time. Some of the product was frozen for further evaluation.

Throughout the activity, the teacher enabled Harry to participate at his own level through careful positioning of support staff, simple visual recipes and actual ingredients, to enable Harry to indicate his choice and 'use' worksheets and recipes to assist working as independently as possible.

Megan

Nicknamed Little Miss Angry, everyone knows when Megan is around! She is very outgoing, loud and tough. No one feels sorry for her – they wouldn't dare! Megan has spina bifida and needs a wheelchair and personal care as well as educational support. She has upset a number of the less experienced Classroom Assistants who find her a real pain. Some of the teachers like her because she is very sparky. If she likes a subject, she works hard – or at least she did until this year.

Megan has to be up very early for her parents to help get her ready for school before the bus comes at 7.50 a.m. She lives out of town and is one of the first to be picked up and one of the last to be dropped off, so she has a longer school day than many of her classmates. Tiredness can be a problem as everything takes her so long to do and involves so much effort.

Now she is fifteen, she has started working towards her GCSEs and has the potential to get several A to Cs particularly in Maths and sciences. She is intelligent but is in danger of becoming disaffected because everything is so much harder for her than for other children. Recently she has lost her temper with a teacher, made cruel remarks to a very sensitive child and turned her wheelchair round so she sat with her back to a supply teacher. She has done no homework for the last few weeks saying that she doesn't see the point as 'no one takes a crip seriously.'

Strategies

- The school needs to identify staff she is on good terms with and make sure she spends time with people she respects.

- Urgent support is needed to minimise the physical effort involved in writing and recording.

- Staff need to discuss things with her instead of talking behind her back and give her some respect.

- The school needs to establish ground rules about behaviour.

- Consider cutting back on number of subjects she is taking.

- Have higher expectations of her.

- Rotate Support Assistants so she doesn't wear them out.

- Talk to parents re health – has there been some deterioration? Problems at home?

- Organise practical work carefully.

- Allow as much independence as possible.

Project example – Corporate identity

Souvenirs and collectables, e.g. T-shirts, 3D signs and models are used to promote events, pop stars, cartoon characters and even schools. Design and make a co-ordinated range of promotional products for a special occasion or a client.

A teacher re-negotiated this DMA with Megan to ask her if she would like to work with a group that was going to be more challenged. Megan enjoys D&T, though she does become tired during long practical sessions. The room is adapted for a wheelchair user and she can access nearly all of the equipment independently. She enjoys food technology because it helps her to work on skills for looking after herself in the future and she is fiercely independent.

The group were going to work directly with an outside client, by e-mail, fax and video/audio conferencing to develop a set of promotional products for an event that was coming up for them.

The teachers supported the group and ensured that they had help when they required it, but once the task was outlined they were left to manage the project for themselves, coming to the teacher with requests when they needed to know something, and reporting back at regular intervals. The group decided on team roles and negotiated their work directly with the company, working independently as far as possible. Megan and the group had to work with a specification requiring that the products were innovative, but also thoroughly tested and of marketable quality. They also designed for an event that was not familiar and required rigorous research from them.

They were ambitious in the range of products they chose and ideas they presented and thus took greater risks and coped with a greater number of variables. The use of CAD/CAM meant Megan produced some high quality products from a design that the pupils worked on as a group.

One of the major contributions that Megan made, as well as helping to design and make the products with the group, was to record the events with a digital camera and put together a powerpoint presentation to the company, showing their prototypes and research.

Megan enjoyed the challenge, and working with an outside company she felt accepted and respected for her ideas and skills.

Steven

'Stevie' is a real charmer – sometimes! He is totally inconsistent: one day, he is full of enthusiasm; the next day, he is very tricky and he needs to be kept on target. He thrives on attention. In primary school, he spent a lot of time sitting by the teacher's desk and seemed to enjoy feeling special. If he sat there he would get on with his work but then as soon as he moved to sit with his friends he wanted to make sure he was the centre of attention.

Now in Year 8, Steven sometimes seems lazy – looking for the easy way out, but at other times he is quite dynamic and has lots of bright ideas. He can't work independently and has a very short attention span. No one has very high expectations of him and he is not about to prove them wrong.

Some of the children don't like him because he can be a bully, but really he is not nasty. He is a permanent lieutenant for some of the tougher boys and does things to win their approval.

He is a thief but mostly he takes silly things, designed to annoy rather than for any monetary value. He was found with someone's library ticket and stole one shoe from the changing rooms during PE.

Since his mother has begun a relationship with a new partner, there has been a deterioration in behaviour and Steven has also been cautioned by police after stealing from a local DIY store. He has just been suspended for throwing a chair at a teacher, but staff suspect this was because he was on a dare. He certainly knows how to get attention.

Strategies

- structured programme with lots of rewards – certificates, merits, etc.

- praise to overcome negative self-image

- success to build confidence, for example using Pro-desktop and electronic portfolios to produce a 'professional looking' result

- information in short chunks

- lots of changes of activity

- some responsibility

- opportunities to give his opinion about products (that he is interested in), help him to feel empowered that he is able to design something to make a difference

- positive support to promote independence

- regular feedback and an opportunity to improve work

- work in a supportive group

Project example – Handheld technologies

Fortunately, Steven really enjoys D&T because it gives him an opportunity to experience success. The teacher began the project by showing Steven examples of handheld technology, encouraging him to be critical about the products and to think of ways that they could be improved. Leading questions were asked to encourage him to reflect critically.

Pupils were given the opportunity of using a computer rather than paper to produce a portfolio, and Steven chose this option. Using an electronic portfolio helped to keep him on task, although many other strategies are also required.

Steven used the Internet to find and download examples of handheld technology and was able to give his opinion of the items in a very basic way. For this project he used examples of existing products to inform his design ideas.

The designs had to be presented in isometric projection and Steven used Pro-desktop to do this. He put forward some design ideas produced on Pro-desktop and evaluated these in a simple manner. At this point he needed visual support (instruction sheets) to help him with pro-desktop as he does not cope well with failure and it was essential to keep him on task. A pictorial guide had been produced using screen captures which Steven could follow in order to produce his design. Using the pictures instead of lots of writing really helped him work independently. The teacher also had a laptop linked to a projector and it was possible to illustrate Pro-desktop step by step so that the pupils could follow the teacher's instructions when they got stuck.

Steven went on to develop his work and propose a final design. This part of the development of his idea was basic but showed that he has some understanding of this aspect of the design process.

Next, the class were shown how to make a product model using Styrofoam. This included the use of a CAM machine to make the buttons. Success at this stage was ensured by managing the classroom so that there were different areas set up for different activities. Pupils were given regular inputs to assist practical work and support was on hand whenever they came to use machinery. During the making stage Steven needed to be closely monitored to ensure he was doing the work required of him and not disturbing anyone else. This was achieved through constant praise and re-assurance. It was also necessary to group him with pupils who would support him rather than antagonise him.

He did complete his product and kept a process diary or step by step guide. As products were being constructed, Steven was encouraged to keep a diary so that he understood which machines were used for various processes. This is a forerunner to pupils planning for themselves. There is a simple evaluation at the end of the project.

In order to maintain interest in the project, each aspect of the work was treated as an end in itself and pupils were given feedback in the form of grades and verbal feedback. Steven was given clear guidance about how his work could be improved and he re-submitted the work at the end of the project for summative assessment.

This was a major achievement for Steven as it was one of the few pieces of work that he managed to complete that year. He said he was really proud of himself, which was good to hear. The key to success was positive support and regular feedback.

Matthew

Matt is a very passive boy. He has no curiosity, no strong likes or dislikes. One teacher said, 'He's the sort of boy who says yes to everything to avoid further discussion but I sometimes wonder if he understands anything.'

Now in Year 9, he is quite a loner. He knows all the children and does not feel uncomfortable with them but is always on the margins. Often in class he sits and does nothing, just stares into space. He is no trouble and indeed if there is any kind of conflict, he absents himself or ignores it. No one knows very much about him as he never volunteers any information. In French, he once said that he had a dog, and one teacher has seen him on the local common with a terrier but no one is sure if it is his.

He does every piece of work as quickly as possible to get it over with. His work is messy and there is no substance to anything he does, which makes it hard for teachers to suggest a way forward, or indeed to find anything to praise. Matthew often looks a bit grubby and is usually untidy. He can be quite clumsy and loses things regularly, but does not bother to look for them. He does less than the minimum.

He is in a low set for maths but stays in the middle. He has problems with most humanities subjects because he has no empathy and no real sense of what is required. When the class went to visit a museum for their work on the Civil War, he was completely unmoved. To him, it was just another building and he could not really link it with the work the class had done in history.

Strategies

- Get parents/carers in to find out if he has any enthusiasms at home.

- Involve him in pair work with a livelier pupil who will 'gee him up' a bit.

- Set up situations where he can make a contribution.

- Set up some one to one sessions with a Support Assistant where he is pushed to respond.

- Get him using technology to improve the appearance of his work, perhaps in a homework club after school.

- Break up D&T projects into small tasks to give regular rewards of success.

- Ask Matthew to adapt a design rather than starting from scratch with a new idea.

- Give support during designing and evaluating stages of projects so that he does not lag behind.

Project example – Design and make a light or lantern

The basic circuit for the light was made and used in science lessons.

The first part of the D&T project was a teacher-led focused practical task to show how to make a timber framework for the light/lantern. The dimensions of the frameworks varied to suit the circuits, which had been mounted onto reclaimed materials. The task was broken down into smaller steps. Matthew received as much support as he needed to do this, so that the product would not be 'lost' because he could not manipulate the timber and card, or measure accurately. Matthew was shown the end result before he started so that he knew what he was aiming for.

The design and make activity was presented to the group when they had made a framework and installed a circuit. Product evaluation activities were used to examine existing torches/lights and lanterns and discuss their purposes. The group identified the fact that they were all comfortable to carry and that they could be switched on and off easily. They also noted that the circuits were protected by the case, and that the bulb was protected by a transparent lens.

Matthew was asked to draw and to annotate the drawing so that he could make a handle for the light. If he had not been able to draw a design, he could have indicated a preference, but he might not have been able to think how to make his design work.

He was also given attractive translucent paper to clad the framework with and so to protect the circuit and the bulb. He was asked to check that he could still reach the switch but he did not have to produce a design to show how he would achieve this.

The products were tested by Matthew for ease of carrying and use of the switch. Matthew evaluated the lantern, first with no support, then as part of a teacher-led writing activity.

Making sure that Matthew had a good end product helped him to feel positive about D&T. Provided some form of informal recording takes place, a lot of adult help does not inflate the assessment of the child's level of achievement. In order to let children working at Matthew's level take part in these interesting class activities, a lot of adult intervention may be needed, allowing the child responsibility for the design and how it is made.

Bhavini

Bhavini has very little useful sight. She uses a stick to get around school and some of the other children make cruel comments about this which she finds very hurtful. She also wears glasses with thick lenses which she hates. On more than one occasion, she has been knocked over in the corridor but she insists that these incidents were accidents and that she is not being bullied. However, her sight is so poor that she may not recognise pupils who pick on her.

Bhavini has a certain amount of specialist equipment such as talking scales in food technology, a CCTV for text books, but now in Year 9, she is always conscious of being different. Her classmates accept her but she is very cut off as she does not make eye contact or see well enough to find people she knows to sit with at break. She spends a lot of time hanging around the support area. Her form tutor has tried to get other children to take her under their wing or to escort her to humanities, which is in another building, but this has bred resentment. She has friends outside school at the local Phab club (Physically handicapped/able-bodied) and has taken part in regional VI Athletics tournaments, although she opts out of sport at school if she can. Some of the teachers are concerned about health and safety issues and there has been talk about her being disapplied from science.

She has a reading age approximately three years behind her chronological age and spells phonetically. Many of the teaching strategies used to make learning more interesting tend to disadvantage her. The lively layout of her French book with cartoons and speech bubbles is a nightmare. Even if she has a page on her CCTV or has a photocopy of the text enlarged she cannot track which bit goes where. At the end of one term she turned up at the support base asking for some work to do because, 'They're all watching videos.'

Strategies

- Her isolation is the key factor and needs addressing most urgently. Make sure she can work on the same projects as the rest of the class.

- She needs to be put in groups with different pupils who will not overwhelm her.

- Work on spelling – core vocabulary and spelling patterns which are not phonic.

- Specialised equipment such as talking weighing scales, talking microwave encourage independence.

- Produce individual resource material that is uncluttered and well spaced.

- Produce instructions on CD/audio for processes and recipes.

Project example – Designing and making a bread product for a teenager

D&T presents particular problems for pupils with visual impairment, as they need a bank of practical skills before being able to design effectively. For Bhavini, it is difficult to think beyond the fact that food products just magically appear on the shelf. It is quite a surprise for her to find out about the complex procedure that is in place to develop a food product. The focus of teaching is on developing much needed life skills, such as finding your way, getting organised independently, getting equipment out and working safely. Thus, D&T plays a rich part in the curriculum for Bhavini and she enjoys learning new things all the time.

The teacher sets up a yeast experiment with balloons on test tubes, to show the right conditions for yeast to grow. Through discussion, pupils identify that there are certain conditions needed to help yeast grow in order for carbon dioxide to be released. Bhavini is able to feel the size of the balloons to identify which test tube is working well. Simple diagrams could be drawn on German film.

The teacher plans a focused practical task making simple bread recipes. This involves listening to instructions, recapping the yeast experiment, and familiarisation of the work area and the talking equipment. The shaping and forming helps to develop a variety of design ideas.

These focused practical tasks are 'mini making' activities to develop skills, add to knowledge and understanding in a practical way, extend experience of different types of breads and create an enjoyable activity that has an end product.

Most pupils will not be able to design and make a new bread product without trying out some existing recipes first. To achieve simple tasks like rubbing in, adding the correct amount of water so that the mixture is ready to squeeze together into a ball before you knead it, is quite difficult for Bhavini. Kneading is fun for most children but she lacks the ability to apply pressure and this has to be practised.

The teacher also sets up a tasting session of existing breads. A variety of different breads are used to develop the organoleptic qualities concerned with tasting but also to enhance pupils' knowledge of the types of ingredients that can be used to make an interesting bread. A strict procedure takes place, recording the sample name, smell, appearance, taste and texture, followed by a drink to cleanse the palate. Bhavini records her results on prepared sheets in Braille or print. This information is used to help her design development.

When designing, Bhavini is encouraged to record her design ideas verbally or to use Wikki Stix®, German film or paper. Less time is spent on recording designs at this stage. She is encouraged to give as much information as possible. She must try to write a simple specification and a list of ingredients needed and be supported if she needs it. During Years 7 and 8, the details for products are simple in order to make sure she is able to achieve the specification in her practical work. This also reinforces her design work – she can feel the real product and compare it to the raised diagram (using Wikki Stix®) – not an easy concept.

Bhavini is able to draw in some detail on paper. As you can see the work is fine for a visually impaired pupil. Improvements could be made but only by using the computer to enhance the quality of the design and written work. However, Bhavini's practical skills are good and she is able to take into consideration the working characteristics of the ingredients used and to shape, form and finish the bread appropriately. When her ICT skills improve she will improve her work, and probably be able to do Entry level/ GCSE later.

Like most pupils Bhavini finds evaluating very hard. Depending on how many weeks are available she may have several attempts at developing the design and recording any changes made as she progresses. Evaluation sheets are provided with structured questions and supporting information.

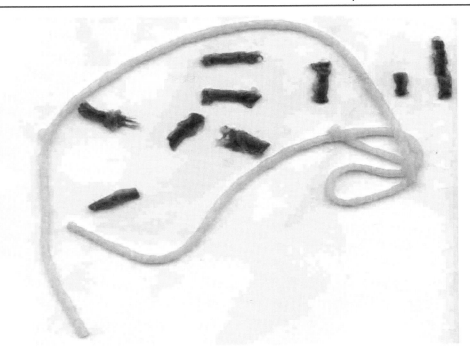

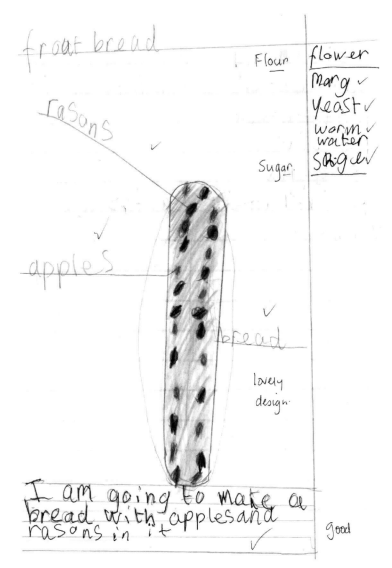

frout bread

Floun flower
Marg ✓
Yeast ✓
worm watter ✓
Sugar SAige ✓

rasons ✓

apples ✓

bread ✓

lovely design.

I am going to make a bread with apples and rasons in it ✓

good

Susan

Susan is a tall, very attractive girl who has been variously labelled as having Asperger's and 'cocktail party syndrome'. She talks fluently but usually about something totally irrelevant. She is very charming and her language is sometimes quite sophisticated, but her ability to use language for school work in Year 10 operates at a much lower level. Her reading is excellent on some levels but she cannot draw inferences from the printed word. If you ask her questions about what she has read, she looks blank, echoes what you have said, looks puzzled or changes the subject – something she is very good at.

She finds relationships quite difficult. She is very popular, especially with the boys in her class. They think she is a laugh. There have been one or two problems with some of the boys in school. Her habit of standing too close to people and her over-familiarity have led to misunderstandings which have upset her. Her best friend Laura is very protective of her and tries to mother her, to the extent of doing some of her work for her so she won't get into trouble.

Her work is limited. In art, all her pictures look the same, very small cramped drawings and she does not like to use paint because 'it's messy.' She finds it very hard to relate to the wider world and sees everything in terms of her own experience. The class has been studying Macbeth and she has not moved beyond saying, 'I don't believe in witches and ghosts.'

Some teachers think she is being wilfully stupid or not paying attention. She seems to be attention seeking as she is very poor at turn taking and shouts out in class if she thinks of something to say or wants to know how to spell a word. When she was younger, she used to retreat under the desk when she was upset and had to be coaxed out. She is still easily offended and cannot bear being teased. She has an answer for everything and, while it may not be sensible or reasonable, there is an underlying logic.

Strategies

- To help her become more independent, allocate carefully structured individual tasks and achievements – give Susan specific group tasks.

- Encourage her to count to 20 before opening her mouth.

- Move her away from Laura.

- Use writing frames and model answers she can base her work on.

- Discuss social issues, body language, appropriate behaviour, etc.

- Keep verbal instructions brief and simple.

- Prepare for changes in advance.

- Make good use of computers, for example designing, adding logos and features to work, evaluation sheets, digital photos and record sheets.

Project example – Design and make a wheeled vehicle

The teacher structured initial tasks to identify the common features and parts of wheeled vehicles and introduce appropriate vocabulary. Susan was asked to collect pictures showing different parts of vehicles and label them for a group display.

The teacher structured focused practical tasks, including making card vehicles from a net, drawing on vehicle parts and adding wheels and axles. The models were then tested by releasing down a ramp. The performances of the vehicles were compared and recorded and the problem of friction discussed. The class used a graph to project results. Susan made a card vehicle from a standard net. She then tested her vehicle for smooth running down a ramp, and recorded her results using RM Starting Graph. This 'mini-making' focused practical task was useful as pupils were able to 'play' with what they made.

Through a teacher-directed focused practical task, Susan made a frame for the chassis from wood strip, adding axle supports, wheels and axles. A full-size plan of the chassis was given to Susan so that she could check the dimensions of the design for the vehicle by placing it on the plan.

The group then went on to design vehicles. Susan drew a full-size plan of the vehicle to be made for her design and make assignment. She used cm squared paper and drew the body of the vehicle within the blue frame already drawn on the paper.

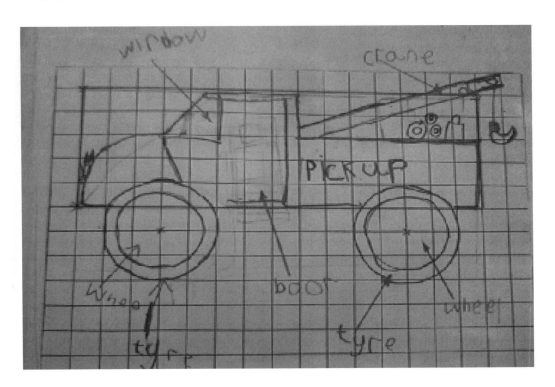

All pupils were able to carry out the making tasks successfully, following practice, and worked fairly accurately. Susan, using the technique she had learned earlier in the focused practical task, made a frame for the chassis from a wooden strip. The vehicle body was made out of plastic foam, and laminated to give the correct depth. Susan made a template from the plan and drew around it onto the foam. She then cut out the shape with a coping saw and hand sanded the model. The body was painted with acrylic paint and details added with pens, metallic paper and card. Susan experimented with using ICT to create logos and names of businesses to add to the vehicle.

Finally, the vehicles were tested. Simple evaluations were carried out on the computer using a template and prompt questions and phrases. Susan's final evaluations were basic and required a heavily structured template with limited choices of phrases from a bank.

Susan required a great deal of structure in the 'vehicles' project. She was able to make simple decisions and choices but found it, in general, very difficult to generate ideas of her own. The introduction of a key, subject-specific, vocabulary encouraged pupils to use the correct terms when speaking and writing.

Evaluation Sheet

Task: to make a wheeled vehicle	
I used __Tools:__ coping saw, safety rule, lynx jointer, handsaw, __Resources:__ wood strip, card triangles, wooden wheels, dowel, plastic tubing, shiny paper, paper clip, thread	**Things that were difficult** • Putting the wheels on • Cutting the body
What I had to do 1. Draw my design on a piece of squared paper. 2. I made a template of my pick-up. 3. I drew round the template on the foam. 4. I cut the body out with a coping saw. 5. I made the chassis from wood strip. 6. I painted the body of my pick-up and put some details on it. 7. I made the crane out of wood strip and a paper clip. 8. I used Word to make labels. 9. I stuck the body on the chassis. 10. I put the axle supports and wheels on my pick-up.	**Final evaluation** I am really pleased with my pick-up. It works well and it goes in a straight line. It was fantastic making the vehicle.

Jenny

Jenny is in Year 7 and has Down's Syndrome. She is a very confident child who has been cherished and encouraged by her mother and older brothers and sisters. She is very assertive and is more than capable of dealing with spiteful comments: 'I don't like it when you call me names. You're cruel and I hate you', but this assertiveness can lead to obstinacy. She is prone to telling teachers that they are wrong!

Jenny has average skills in reading and writing but her work tends to be unimaginative and pedestrian. She enjoys biology but finds the rest of the science curriculum hard going. She has started to put on weight and tries to avoid PE. She has persuaded her mother to provide a note saying that she tires easily but staff know that she is a bundle of energy and is an active member of an amateur theatre group which performs musicals. She has a good singing voice and enjoys dancing.

She went to a local nursery and primary school and fitted in well. She always had some one to sit next to and was invited to all the best birthday parties. Teachers and other parents frequently praised her and she felt special.

Now in secondary school, everything has changed. Some of her friends from primary school have made new friendships and don't want to spend so much time with her. She is very hurt by this and feels excluded. She is also struck by how glamorous some of the older girls look and this has made her more self-conscious.

Strategies

- Talk to parents about diet and exercise and find a way of making Susan feel more attractive.

- Encourage new groupings in class so she gets to meet other children from different feeder schools.

- Pair her up with a child who has better imaginative/empathy skills but weaker literacy, so they can support each other.

- Be aware that too much one-to-one support can be counter-productive: support independence as much as possible.

- Reinforce discussions with pictures and real products; keep listening activities short.

- Use short, clear instructions.

Project example – Design and make a pencil case

The teacher asked the class to work on a project to design and make a textile container or carrier, such as a pencil case, that could be manufactured in batches or as a single item. Pupils developed a basic design that could be varied or personalised for particular clients. The assignment required them to justify their decisions about materials and methods of making. The part that appealed to Jenny was being able to make something that she could take home and use.

The teacher organised a class discussion on the subject, 'Where do new design ideas come from?'. The class used information from designers and older pupils to help develop their ideas. The teacher described to the pupils how designers record their thoughts, design ideas and explorations, for example how they use sketchbooks, moodboards, collages, drawings or collections of inspiring photographs. She showed the pupils good and poor examples of recording and explained that they would need to choose the best methods for their design work.

Jenny was asked to collect images, pictures, photos and samples of fabric that interested her to put in her sketchbook for designing later. The teacher showed Jenny how she could use these ideas imaginatively: 'Look at this postcard of a beach: you could try to match the colours of the sea . . . Look at the pattern on this fabric closely: What do you see? What shapes are there?'

During focused practical tasks, the teacher showed the pupils examples of how manufacturing aids (for example, printing blocks and patterns) can be made or used to help with single or batch production. The teacher discussed how to design and make identical parts in a batch. The teacher also made samples of seams, and showed the group possible fastenings. Jenny was given time to practise these to reinforce basic sewing skills, and to make sure the end product was successful.

Jenny generated some ideas during a whole-class discussion and identified possible information sources, such as magazines, from which she cut out examples of existing products. Her designs did not really move from copying images that existed already, but she did talk about price for materials and who might buy her kind of pencil case.

The teacher showed Jenny printing methods she could use to apply colour to her design and she tried some out. She took users' views into account during the testing of materials with a group of other pupils, in order to identify the most suitable fabric to use.

Jenny communicated alternative ideas for pencil cases through annotated sketches; she also showed the design in different colours. She then selected the best combination to use in her final design drawing. The teacher encouraged Jenny to present her ideas during a lesson plenary to the rest of the class, with several other pupils, so that Jenny had a chance to speak to others.

Jenny followed a basic step-by-step plan outlining the order of her work and the equipment to be used. She worked with a variety of materials and components with help from adults. She could choose tools for the job from a limited range.

She was not able to focus her final evaluation well, but she identified what worked well and what could be improved.